PREFACE

This volume is the second in a series of four, each of which has been planned to cover one stage in the composition work of the secondary-school course. These books have been designed to supply material adapted as exactly as possible to the capacity of the pupils. Most of the exercises which they contain have been devised with the idea of reproducing in an elementary form the methods of self-instruction which have been employed by successful writers from Homer to Kipling. Nearly all of them have been subjected to the test of actual classroom use on a large scale. They may be used independently or as supplementary to a more formal textbook. Each volume contains rather more work than an ordinary class can do in one hundred recitations.

In each volume will be found exercises that involve each of the four forms of discourse; but emphasis is placed in Book I on description, in Book II on narration, in Book III on exposition, and in Book IV on argumentation. Similarly, while stress is laid in Book I on letter-writing, in Book II on journalism, in Book III on literary effect, and in Book IV on the civic aspects of composition, all of these phases of the subject receive attention in each volume.

In every lesson of each book provision is made for oral work: first, because it is an end valuable in itself; second, because it is of incalculable use in preparing the ground for written work; third, because it can be made to give the pupil a proper and powerful motive for writing with care; and, fourth, because, when employed with discretion, it lightens the teacher's burden without impairing his efficiency.

Composition is not writing. Writing is only one step in composition. The gathering of material, the organization of material, criticism, revision, publication, and the reaction that follows publication are therefore in these volumes given due recognition.

The quotation at the head of each chapter and the poem at the end are designed to furnish that stimulus to the will and the imagination without which great practical achievement [Page iv] is impossible. On the other hand, the exercises are all designed on the theory that the sort of idealism which has no practical results is a snare. Indeed, the books might be characterized as an effort to find a useful compromise between those warring types of educational theory which are usually characterized by the words "academic" and "vocational."

The specific subject of this volume is newspaper writing. The author has himself had enough experience in practical newspaper work to appreciate the difficulties and to respect the achievements of the journalist. He knows that editors must print what people will buy. It seems probable, therefore, that instruction in the elementary principles of newspaper writing, in addition to producing good academic results, may lead pupils to read the papers critically, to discriminate between the good and the bad, and to demand a better quality of journalism than it is now possible for editors to offer. If this happens, the papers will improve. The aim of this book is therefore social as well as academic. It is also vocational. Some of the boys and girls who study it will learn from its pages the elements of the arts of proof-reading and reporting well enough to begin, by virtue of the skill thus acquired, to earn their bread and butter.

For the chapters on advertising I am indebted to Mr. Karl Murchey, of the Cass Technical High School of Detroit, Michigan. Mr. John V. Brennan, Miss Grace Albert, and Miss Eva Kinney, of the Detroit Northwestern High School, have rendered me invaluable help by suggestions, by proof-reading, and by trying out the exercises in their classes. Mr. C. C. Certain, of Birmingham, Alabama, and Mr. E. H. Kemper McComb, of the Technical High School, Indianapolis, by hints based on their own wide experience and ripe scholarship, have enabled me to avoid numerous pitfalls. My thanks are due also to Mr. Francis W. Daire, of the *Newark News*, and Mr. C. B. Nicolson, of the *Detroit Free Press*, who have given me the benefit of their experience as practical newspaper men. Above all, I am indebted to my friend, Mr. Henry P. Hetherington, of the *Detroit Journal*, whose untimely death in June, 1914, deprived me of a never-failing source of wisdom and a critic to whose ripe judgment I owe more than I know how to describe.

E. L. M.

CHAPTER I
THE NEWSPAPER

"Truth is the highest thing that man may keep."

CHAUCER.

I. Introduction

THE object of this book is to teach high-school boys and girls how to write plain newspaper English. Next to letter-writing, this is at once the simplest and the most practical form of composition. The pupil who does preëminently well the work outlined in this volume may become a proof-reader, a reporter, an editor, or even a journalist. In other words, the student of this book is working on a practical bread-and-butter proposition. He must remember, however, that the lessons it contains are elementary. They are only a beginning. And even this beginning can be made only by the most strenuous and persistent exertions. English is not an easy subject. It is the hardest subject in the curriculum. To succeed in English three things are required: (1) Work; (2) *Work*; (3) WORK.

II. The Newspaper

The modern city newspaper is a complicated machine. At its head is usually a general manager, who may be one of its owners. Directly responsible to him are the business manager, the superintendent of the mechanical department, and the managing editor.

[Page 2] The business manager has under him three sub-departments: (1) Advertising; (2) Circulation; (3) Auditing. To the first of these is entrusted the duty of taking care of those small advertisements which, owing to the fact that each occupies only a line or two, are called "liners"; the management of a corps of solicitors; and the maintenance of amicable relations with the business men of the community. The circulation department includes not only the management of local and foreign circulation, but also the collection of money from subscribers, dealers, and newsboys. The auditor keeps the books, has charge of the cash, and manages the payroll.

The superintendent of the mechanical department has three subordinates. These are the foreman of the composing-room, the foreman of the pressroom, and the foreman of the stereotyping-room. Each, of course, always has several assistants and often many.

The managing editor has charge of the collection and distribution of news. He has no routine duties, but is responsible for the conduct of his subordinates, for the character of the paper, and for its success as a business enterprise. The relation of the paper to the public is in his keeping. Not infrequently he has serious differences of opinion with the business manager, especially when he publishes news which does not please important advertisers. Among his chief occupations are devising methods of getting news and avoiding libel suits. The subordinates who report directly to him are the writers of special columns, the cartoonists, the editorial writers, the editor of the Sunday paper, and the assistant managing editor, or news editor. It is with the latter and his staff that we are at present chiefly concerned.

[Page 3] The news editor, or night editor, as he is called on a morning paper, has charge of all the routine that is involved in the production of the paper. Its make-up is in his hands. An autocrat on space and place, he is seldom praised, but must take the blame for everything that goes wrong. Under him are: (1) A telegraph editor, whose business it is to handle news from outside the State; (2) a State editor, who directs as best he may a horde of local correspondents who represent the paper in the rural and semi-rural districts; (3) one or more "rewrite men" or copy-readers, whose business it is to write out the news sent in by telephone, to correct the errors of illiterate reporters, and to rewrite articles when necessary; and (4) the city editor.

This last functionary is frequently the most important man on the paper. He is responsible for gathering nearly all of the original news that goes into its columns. To be able to do this he must have a wide and exact knowledge of the people and the history of the city. He works like a slave; and the reporters, who are under his direct control, find in him a stern but appreciative taskmaster.

These reporters, or news-gatherers, lead a strenuous but not unhappy life. It is somewhat like that of the huntsman, their business being to stalk news, which is perhaps the biggest and certainly the most elusive game which the world produces. Their lives are sometimes, their liberty oftener, and their jobs always, in danger. If one of them permits a rival paper to get a "scoop," he is apt to find himself in the situation of the warrior described in Shakespeare's sonnet:

[Page 4]

> "The painful warrior, famousëd for fight,
>   After a thousand victories once foiled,
> Is from the book of honour razëd quite,
>   And all the rest forgot for which he toiled."

Some reporters hunt everywhere; others are assigned to special "beats." Of the latter the city hall is the most important, but the central police station yields the largest number of good stories, because it is there that tales of human folly, crime, and tragedy are most promptly known. On most papers the law courts, politics, sport, drama, religion, education, marine affairs, and society provide other "beats."

The organization thus briefly sketched is fairly typical, though by no means universal. The outline on page 5 may make it a little clearer.

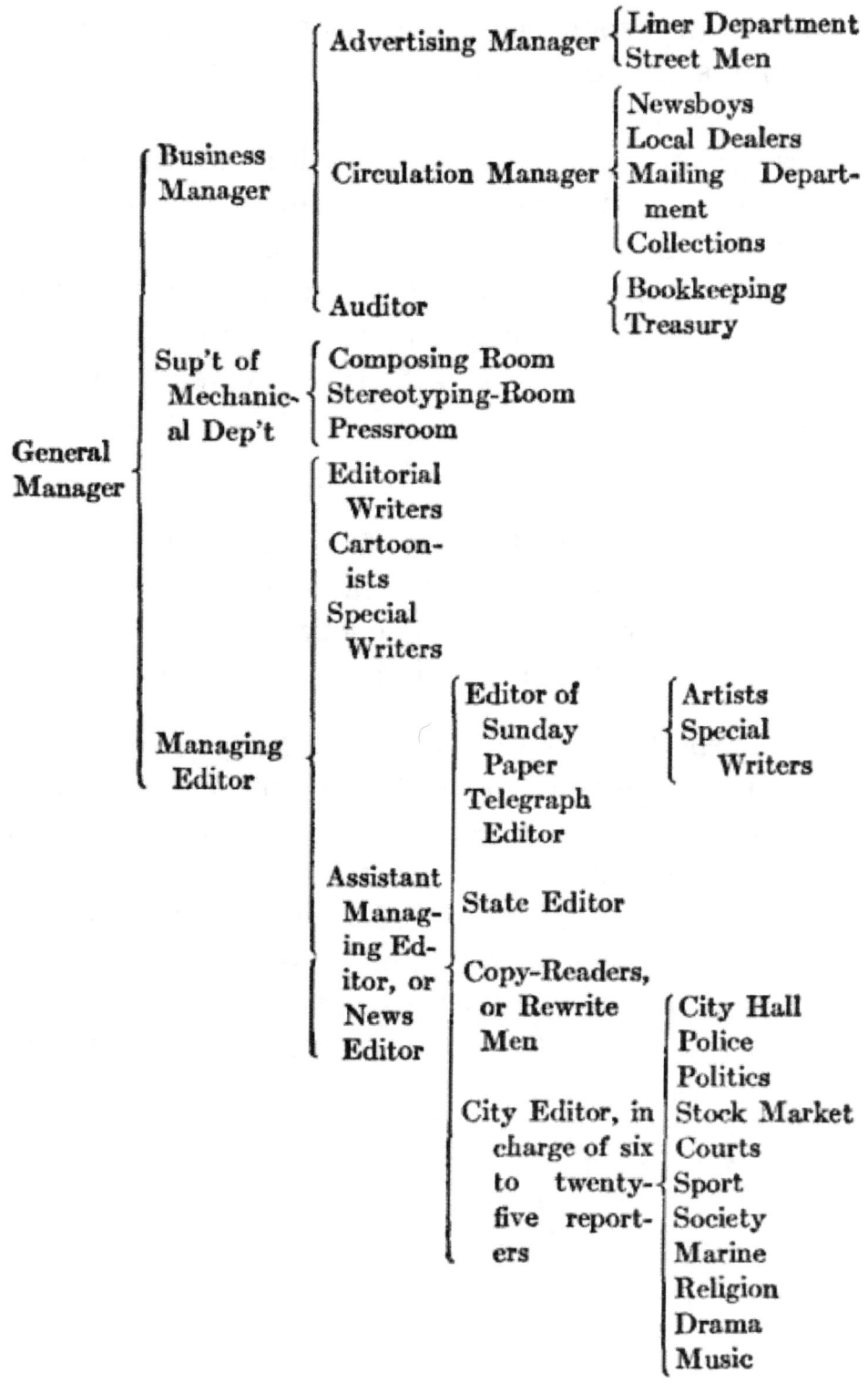

[Textual representation of diagram.]

Good reporters are not numerous. The reason is that, to succeed in this work, a man or a woman must be able to gather news and to write. There are plenty of people who can do either, but few who can do both.

In order to get news one must be physically tireless, fond of adventure, persistent, unabashed, polite, courageous, and resourceful in the highest degree. To the successful reporter an impossibility is only an opportunity in disguise. In his lexicon there is no such word as "fail." He must know how to make and keep friends. He must have that kind of originality which is called "initiative." Above all, he must be scrupulously honest. He must be actuated by a fixed determination to get the news, the whole news, and nothing but the news.

In order to write well one must be able to spell, punctuate, and capitalize; know the laws of grammar and how to apply them; be familiar with the principles of rhetoric; and have a wide acquaintance with good [Page 6] books. These qualities are not usually found in company with those which make a successful news-gatherer. A person who has both is therefore worth his weight in gold to a newspaper. The fact that this combination of qualities is so rare leads many papers to employ special rewrite men whose business it is to put into good English the raw material furnished by the news-gatherer.

One other newspaper functionary remains to be noticed, the writer of editorials. News items are confined to facts. Editorials contain expressions of opinion. Everybody reads news, because it speaks for itself. Editorials are designed to mould public opinion. Unless they are characterized by extreme good sense or brilliancy, nobody heeds them, though, if he makes a mistake in one, the writer of editorials is apt to conclude that everybody reads them. The writer of editorials must therefore be a person of exceptional qualifications.

III. Class Organization

For the present the teacher of the class studying this book may act as city editor and the pupils as reporters. Later, perhaps, a more formal organization may be effected, with pupils as managing editor, assistant managing editor, city editor, etc.

IV. Newspaper Coöperation

The editor of the local paper will probably be willing to print any really good material that the class produces. If possible, an arrangement for this purpose should be made with him. It is also possible that he may be willing to supplement this chapter by talking to the class.

[Page 7] V. Topics for Oral Discussion

1. What Is a Newspaper?
2. The History of Journalism.
3. Why is a Study of Journalistic Writing Practical?
4. The Organization of a Newspaper.
5. The Managing Editor.
6. The Composing-room.
7. The Business Manager.
8. The Assistant Managing Editor.
9. The Telegraph Editor.
10. The State Editor.
11. The City Editor.
12. The Reporter.
13. "Beats."
14. "Scoops."
15. Editorials.
16. The Gospel of Work.

VI. Suggested Reading

Kipling's *The Man Who Would Be King* and *The Light That Failed*.

VII. Memorize

A PSALM OF LIFE

Tell me not, in mournful numbers,
    Life is but an empty dream,
For the soul is dead that slumbers
    And things are not what they seem.

Life is real, life is earnest,
    And the grave is not its goal;
"Dust thou art, to dust returnest,"
    Was not spoken of the soul.

Not enjoyment and not sorrow
    Is our destined end or way;
But to act, that each to-morrow
    Find us farther than to-day.

Art is long, and Time is fleeting,
    And our hearts, though stout and brave,
Still, like muffled drums, are beating
    Funeral marches to the grave.

In the world's broad field of battle,
    In the bivouac of Life,
Be not like dumb, driven cattle!
    Be a hero in the strife!

(*Continued on Page 13.*)

← Contents

CHAPTER II
NEWS ITEMS

"Facts are stubborn things."

Le Sage.

I. Assignment

Find and report some unusual and interesting thing that has been made or done by boys or girls. Do not get your information from literature. Get it from life. Above all, don't make it up. It must be fact, not fiction.

When the city editor gives a reporter an assignment, he does not expect to answer questions. The reporter's business is to give the city editor copy, not to rely on him for information. The reporter who does not promptly learn this fact soon ceases to be a reporter.

II. Getting the Facts

In all writing the gathering of material is more important than any other one thing. In reportorial work it is almost all-important. Almost anybody can tell a story if he has the facts. Energy, persistent politeness, and a pair of stout legs are more essential in reporting than is a large vocabulary. The pursuit of news is always a fascinating and sometimes a dangerous game. If you do not believe this, read *Fighting in Flanders*, by E. Alexander Powell; or *The Events Man*, by Richard Barry. Above everything else, remember that the most uncompromising adherence to facts is essential.

Do not make the mistake of supposing that newspaper men fail to recognize the importance of telling the exact truth. They strive constantly and strenuously to do so. In the office of the *New York World* there used to be, and probably still is, a placard on which Joseph Pulitzer had printed these three words: "Accuracy, Accuracy, ACCURACY." All reporters strive constantly to be accurate. If they do not always succeed, it is due to the difficulty of the task. They have to work fast lest the news grow cold. Usually they write in the midst of an uproar. When you are disposed to find fault with them by reason of their carelessness, remember that Sir Walter Raleigh, unable to determine the facts concerning a quarrel that occurred under his own window, concluded that his chance of telling the truth about events that happened centuries previous was small.

III. Writing

In preparing manuscript the typewriter in these days is almost indispensable. The value to a reporter of a course in typewriting is therefore obvious. It is also obvious that copy must be letter-perfect. Before it can be printed, it must be entirely free from mistakes in spelling, punctuation, capitalization, and the other essentials of good usage.

IV. Model

The following article is clipped from a New York daily. In what it says and leaves unsaid it is an excellent model.

FARTHEST NORTH IS RIGHT HERE IN TOWN

Hundreds of persons were attracted yesterday to Brook Avenue, near One Hundred and Forty-ninth Street, to inspect the handiwork in snow of three fourteen-year-old boys.

They had built a thick-walled cottage, 25 feet high and with 15 × 16 feet ground dimensions. Roof and walls, inside and out, had been smoothed; and a coat of water had turned the snow house into a shimmering glaze.

The interior was divided into four rooms, all bearing out the truthfulness of the sign tacked up without, which read: "House to let, three rooms and bath." Even the bath, modeled in snow, was there. Rugs, tables, chairs, and sofas made the Esquimau edifice cozy within; and an oil stove kept eggs and coffee sizzling merrily at dinner time.

The builders were three days at their task. They are Tom Brown, of No. 516 East One Hundred and Forty-seventh Street; Arthur Carraher, of No. 430 Brook Avenue; and Walter Waller, of No. 525 East One Hundred and Forty-fifth Street.

V. Notes and Queries

1. State the reason for the use of each capital letter and each mark of punctuation in the model.
2. Tell whether each sentence is simple, complex, or compound.
3. Explain the syntax of each adverb in the model.
4. Point out three words or phrases that have color, character, or distinction.
5. What is the subject of each paragraph?
6. Are the "Four W's" sufficiently indicated? Point them out.
7. Study the heading. The art of writing good headings is almost as difficult as that of writing good poetry, which it resembles in that, as the poet is limited to a certain number of syllables, the writer of headlines is limited to a fixed number of letters.

VI. Suggested Time Schedule

Monday

Discuss Sections I, II, and III of this chapter. Send the class to the board and dictate the model as an exercise in spelling, punctuation, and capitalization. Review last week's work.

Tuesday

Recitation on Notes and Queries.

[Page 12] *Wednesday*

Oral Composition: i.e., each pupil will bring to class his news article—not written but in his head—and be prepared to deliver it to the class as if he were a reporter dictating to a stenographer or telephoning his report to his paper.

Thursday

Profiting by Wednesday's discussion, the pupils will write their articles and hand them to the teacher, who will proof-read them and return them on Monday.

Friday

Public Speaking—Organize the class as a club. Let the officers arrange a program consisting of declamations, debates, essays, dialogues, etc. This day may also be used for the reading of the best articles that members of the class have written.

VII. Organization of Material

After you get your story, you must decide on a plan for its discussion. This will depend largely on its nature. Indeed, the plan and the style of any piece of writing are to the material as are the clothes to the body. They must fit the body. The body determines their shape.

The model in Section IV is a bit of exposition composed partly of description and partly of narration. Its framework is as follows:

Par. 1. The "Four W's":
    Who = hundreds of people; What = handiwork in snow;
    When = yesterday; Where = Brook Avenue near One
    Hundred and Forty-ninth Street.

Par. 2. The Exterior of the House.

Par. 3. The Interior.

Par. 4. The Architects.

VIII. Some Possible Subjects

1. The Gas Engine that Jack built.
2. A Profitable Garden.
3. [Page 13] How a Boy earned his Education.
4. A Cabinet.
5. How to bind Books.
6. Stocking and keeping an Aquarium.
7. How to build a Flatboat.
8. How to make Dolls from Corn-Husks.
9. Metallic Band Work.
10. A Sled made of Ice.
11. Silk Culture.
12. Chickens.
13. A Good Notebook.
14. A Sketch-Book.
15. A Successful Composition.
16. Skees.
17. A Paper Boat.
18. Toys made in the Manual Training Rooms.
19. A Hat.
20. A Dress.
21. The best subject of all, however, is none of these, but one that the pupil finds himself.

IX. Suggested Reading

Elbert Hubbard's *A Message to Garcia*.

X. Memorize

A PSALM OF LIFE (*continued from Page 7*)

Trust no future, howe'er pleasant!
   Let the dead Past bury its dead!
Act, act in the living Present!
   Heart within and God o'erhead!

Lives of great men all remind us,
   We can make our lives sublime,
And, departing, leave behind us
   Footprints on the sands of time;

Footprints that perhaps another,
   Sailing o'er life's solemn main,
A forlorn and shipwrecked brother,
   Seeing, shall take heart again.

[Page 14]
Let us, then, be up and doing,
   With a heart for any fate;
Still achieving, still pursuing,
   Learn to labor and to wait.
HENRY WADSWORTH LONGFELLOW.

TO TEACHERS. At this point a review of Chapter V, "Proof-Reading" and Chapter VI, "The Correction of Themes," of *Practical English Composition*, Book I, will be found an invaluable exercise.

← Contents

CHAPTER III
BIOGRAPHICAL NOTICES

> "Lives of great men all remind us
> We can make our lives sublime."
>
> Longfellow.

I. Assignment

Write a biographical note of about two hundred words concerning a citizen who has just come into public notice.

II. Obtaining the Facts

If the subject of the note is already distinguished, the facts can usually be collected from books and periodicals. Poole's *Index of Periodical Literature* will point the way. Most newspapers keep an indexed mass of biographical material, which, of course, is at a reporter's disposal. When these sources fail, the man himself must be interviewed, which is a task that requires tact, politeness, persistency, a good memory, and a clear idea of the character and quantity of the information needed.

III. Models

I

James McHenry was born in Ireland, 1753; came to Philadelphia, 1771; studied medicine under Dr. Benjamin Rush; served in the Revolutionary War as surgeon; became Washington's secretary, 1778; sat in Congress, 1783–86; was a member of the Constitutional Convention; was Secretary of War under Washington and Adams, 1796–1801; and died in Baltimore, 1816.

His most conspicuous public service was rendered in inducing Maryland to ratify the Constitution. [Page 16] Fort McHenry, the bombardment of which in 1814 inspired Francis Scott Key to write the *Star-Spangled Banner*, was named in McHenry's honor.

II

Alexander Hamilton is one of those great Americans of whose services to the nation no American can afford to be ignorant. As a soldier in the Revolution, no man possessed more of Washington's confidence. To him as much as to any one man was due the movement that resulted in the formation of the Constitution; he took a leading part in the debates of the Convention; and the ratification of the Constitution was brought about largely by the *Federalist,* a paper in which he so ably interpreted the provisions of that instrument that it has ever since been regarded as one of the world's political classics. As Secretary of the Treasury under Washington he performed wonders; Daniel Webster said of his work in this office: "He rent the rock of the national resources, and abundant streams of revenue gushed forth. He touched the dead corpse of Public Credit, and it sprung upon its feet." He was born in Nevis, one of the West Indies, in 1757, and was mortally wounded by Aaron Burr in a duel, 1804, at Weehawken, New Jersey.

IV. Organization of Material

Models I and II illustrate two types of biographical notes. That about James McHenry consists of three sentences, which give: (1) A chronological survey of his life; (2) a statement of his chief public service; (3) the fact by which he is most likely to be remembered by the casual reader. It is a good brief form to use in writing about most men and women. Model II is better if the subject is remarkable for many achievements. Its structure is as follows: (1) A keynote sentence; (2), (3), (4) three illustrations of the fact stated in (1); (5) dates. The same principles apply to notices of living people. In writing use one model or the [Page 17] other; do not deviate from them, unless you first find a better model, and can persuade your teacher that it is better.

V. Exercises

1. Reduce some biography which you have read and enjoyed to a biographical note of two hundred words.
2. Write a biographical note of two hundred words about a living person of national reputation.
3. Write a biographical note of two hundred words about a living person of state or city reputation.
4. Write a biographical note about the school janitor, the school engineer, a member of your own family, your hired man, your maid, or any other interesting person from whom you can extract the desired information.

VI. Suggested Reading

Carl Schurz's *Life of Abraham Lincoln*.

VII. Memorize

THE SEVEN AGES OF MAN

All the world's a stage,
And all the men and women merely players.
They have their exits and their entrances;
And one man in his time plays many parts,
His acts being seven ages. At first the infant,

Mewling and puking in the nurse's arms.
And then the whining school-boy, with his satchel
And shining morning face, creeping like snail
Unwillingly to school. And then the lover,
Sighing like furnace, with a woful ballad
Made to his mistress's eyebrow. Then a soldier,
Full of strange oaths and bearded like the pard;
Jealous in honor, sudden and quick in quarrel,
Seeking the bubble reputation
Even in the cannon's mouth. And then the justice,
In fair round belly with good capon lined,
With eyes severe and beard of formal cut,
Full of wise saws and modern instances;
And so he plays his part. The sixth age shifts
Into the lean and slippered pantaloon,
With spectacles on nose and pouch on side;
His youthful hose, well saved, a world too wide
For his shrunk shank, and his big manly voice,
Turning again toward childish treble, pipes
And whistles in his sound. Last scene of all,
That ends this strange eventful history,
Is second childishness and mere oblivion,
Sans teeth, sans eyes, sans taste, sans everything.
   SHAKESPEARE, *As You Like It*, Act II,
          Scene 7.

CHAPTER IV
REPORTING ACCIDENTS

"The truth, the whole truth, and nothing but the truth."

I. Assignment

Report an accident which you have seen. The object of this exercise and those which are to follow is threefold:

1. Vocational—to begin to teach the art of reporting, and hence perhaps lay a foundation for students' earning a living.
2. Ethical—to show all the pupils how a report should be made and thus give them a standard by which to measure newspapers.
3. Artistic—to teach all how to write modern English clearly, simply, and correctly.

II. Model

This is a report of an accident on a city street, witnessed by a reporter, and telephoned to a colleague at the newspaper office.

> With a crash that could be heard for blocks, a high-powered touring car, owned and driven by Mrs. William J. Sheldon, wife of the millionaire gum manufacturer, who lives at East Boulevard and Clifton Drive, collided late last night with a heavy milk wagon at Payne Avenue and East 30th St. Both Mrs. Sheldon and John Goldrick, 656 East 105th St., driver of the milk wagon, escaped injury, except for a few minor cuts and bruises.
>
> Mrs. Sheldon was driving east on Payne Avenue on the way to the Pennsylvania Station at Euclid Avenue to

meet her [Page 20] husband, who was coming from New York. The street at Payne Avenue and East 30th St. had just been flushed; and, when Mrs. Sheldon endeavored to turn out toward the car tracks to avoid hitting Goldrick's wagon, which was just turning into Payne Avenue, the car skidded and side-swiped the wagon.

One wheel of the machine and the mud guard were torn loose, while glass from the shattered wind-shield rained over Mrs. Sheldon as she strove desperately to twist the wheel. Goldrick was hurled from his seat, landing in the back of the wagon, which was piled high with cases of milk bottles. The horses were thrown from their feet by the shock.

Mrs. Sheldon and Goldrick were extricated from the wreckage and conveyed to the office of Dr. W. A. Masters, Payne Avenue and East 32d St., where their injuries were dressed. Later they were taken to their homes.

III. Suggested Time Schedule

Monday—Dictation of Model and Study of Last Week's Errors.
Tuesday—Notes and Queries.
Wednesday—Oral Composition—e.g., Telephoning.
Thursday—Written Composition.
Friday—Public Speaking.

IV. Notes, Queries, and Exercises

1. How many paragraphs are there in the report in Section II?
2. What is the subject of each?
3. The object?

4. Point out the "Four W's."

5. State why each capital and each mark of punctuation in the model is used.

6. Tell whether each sentence is simple, complex, or compound.

7. Find in the model an adverbial phrase, an adverb, a noun used adverbially, a noun in apposition, a clause modifying a verb, a participle modifying the subject of a verb, a non-restrictive clause, and a clause used as an adjective.

8. [Page 21] Point out four words or phrases that give color to the story.

9. Write an appropriate heading for the model.

V. Oral Composition

Prepare a report of some accident which you have yourself seen or which has been described to you by an eye-witness. Be sure to get into the report in the proper order the "Four W's," the cause, and the result. Note that a good story usually consists of three parts:

1. The Previous Situation.
2. What Happened = The Climax.
3. The Result = The Dénouement.

These are all in the model, but 2 is put first because it is most important. Observe the order of the model. Each member of the class will have a chance to make his report orally, and it will be subjected to the analysis of the class and teacher, who will blame or praise it according to its deserts. The reporter must defend himself, if attacked. Each pupil will therefore in turn play the rôle of a reporter, telephoning a story to headquarters while the class and teacher enact the part of the city editor.

VI. Written Composition

After the process outlined in Section IV of this chapter has shown the reporter how to go about the job, the report is to be written, proof-read by the teacher, corrected by the reporter, and rewritten until it is letter-perfect.

VII. Suggested Reading

Kipling's *007* in *The Day's Work*.

VIII. Memorize

SUNSHINE

> Think every morning when the sun peeps through
> The dim leaf-latticed windows of the grove
> How jubilant the happy birds renew
> Their long melodious madrigals of love;
> And, when you think of this, remember too
> 'Tis always morning somewhere, and above
> The awakening continents from shore to shore
> Somewhere the birds are singing evermore.
> LONGFELLOW, *The Birds of Killingworth*.

[Page 23] CHAPTER V
CONSTRUCTIVE NEWSPAPER WRITING

"The drying up a single tear has more
Of honest fame than shedding seas of gore."
                                                    LORD BYRON.

I. Introduction

THE worst thing about most news articles is that they tell of destruction, failure, and tragedy instead of construction, success, and happiness. If one were to judge from the papers, one would be forced to conclude that the world is rapidly advancing from civilization to barbarism. To test the truth of this assertion, you have only to examine almost any current newspaper. A man may labor honorably and usefully for a generation without being mentioned; but if he does or says a foolish thing, the reporters flock to him as do cats to a plate of cream. The reason is obvious. Tragedy is more exciting than any other form of literature; it contains thrills; it sells papers. However, aside from the fact that the publication of details concerning human folly and misfortune is often cruel and unjust to the sufferers, its influence upon the public is debasing in the same way, if not in the same degree, as public executions were debasing.

Newspaper writing should, therefore, deal with progress rather than with retrogression. Most newspaper men admit that this is true, but declare that the public will not buy the kind of papers which all sensible people approve. Just as soon as such papers can be made to pay, they say, we shall have them. One [Page 24] of the objects of this course is to create a taste for constructive rather than destructive newspapers.

As an exercise tending to produce this result, the student should each day examine the local paper for the purpose of ascertaining how many columns of destruction and how many of construction it contains. The result should be reported to the class and thence to the papers as news.

There are three kinds of items which boys and girls can write and which are constructive. These are:

1. Items dealing with progress.

2. Humorous stories.

3. Items based on contrast.

The work this week will be on the first of these.

II. Models

I

St. Louis, Feb. 22.—L. C. Phillips will plant 1,000 acres of his southeast Missouri land in sunflowers this year as a further demonstration that this plant can be cultivated with profit on land where other crops may not thrive so well. Phillips has been experimenting for several years in the culture of sunflowers, whose seed, when mixed with other seed, makes excellent chicken and hog feed. Last year he planted nearly 100 acres in sunflowers. The cost of planting and harvesting is about $6 an acre, he says, and the returns from $35 to $48.

II

Halifax, N.S., Dec. 25.—One of the most extraordinary endowments bestowed by nature on any land is enjoyed by the fortunate group of counties round the head of the Bay of Fundy, Nova Scotia.

Along the shores of this bay there are great stretches of meadow land covered with rich grass and dotted with barns. These meadows have been brought into existence by the power of the tides in the Bay of Fundy, which have no [Page 25] parallel elsewhere on the globe. There is sometimes a difference of sixty feet between the levels of the water at low and at high tide. The tide sweeps in with a rush, carrying with it a vast amount of solid material scoured out of its channel.

The accumulated deposits of the ages have produced a soil seventy or eighty feet deep. Owing to its peculiarities, this meadow land retains its fertility in a marvelous way, producing heavy crops of hay annually without diminution and without renewal for an indefinite number of years.

When renewal is desired it is only necessary to open a dike, which allows the tide to flood the land again and leave a fresh deposit of soil.

III

WASHINGTON, Dec. 25.—Michigan holds sixth place among the States in the value of its mineral production, with an output in 1912 valued at $180,062,486, according to the United States Geological Survey, its prominence being due to its great wealth in copper and iron. Ranking second only to Minnesota in the production of iron ore, it is third in the production of copper, being exceeded only by Arizona and Montana. It also stands first in the production of salt, bromine, calcium chloride, graphite, and sand lime brick.

In 1911 Michigan's production of iron ore was 8,945,103 long tons, valued at $23,810,710, and in 1912 it increased to 12,717,468 long tons, valued at $28,003,163.

The production of copper in Michigan, the value of which in the last two years has exceeded that of the output of iron ore, amounted in 1912 to 218,138,408 pounds, valued at $135,992,837, a decrease in quantity, but an increase in value of over $8,000,000.

The mining of copper in Michigan is of prehistoric origin, the metal having been used by the North American Indians before the advent of the white man. The records since 1810, or for a little more than 100 years, show that the total production of copper in Michigan from that date to the close of 1912 has amounted to over 5,200,000,000 pounds, which is about 30 per cent of the total output of the United States.

[Page 26] **III. Oral Composition**

All three of these items are evidently condensations of longer articles. The writers have boiled down a vast amount of material into the form in which it here appears. The student will find similar material in abundance in *The Literary Digest,* in *The Scientific American,* in *The National Geographical Magazine,* in many government reports, and in almost any daily newspaper. In preparing for this exercise he should observe the following steps:

1. Find his material.
2. Boil it down, to the size desired, which is a most useful exercise of the judgment.
3. Make a careful framework, in doing which the models will be useful.
4. Get the whole so well in mind that he can present it fluently. Hesitation should not be tolerated.

IV. Suggested Time Schedule

Monday—Dictation.
Tuesday—Notes and Queries.
Wednesday—Oral Composition.
Thursday—Written Composition.
Friday—Public Speaking.

V. Notes, Queries, and Exercises.

1. Write an appropriate heading for each item.
2. Point out the "Four W's" in each.
3. Tell whether each sentence is simple, compound, or complex.
4. Explain the syntax of the nouns in Model I, the pronouns in II, the verbs in III.
5. Explain the location of St. Louis, Halifax, Nova Scotia, the Bay of Fundy, Washington, Michigan, Minnesota, Arizona, and Montana.
6. [Page 27] Where is the copper country of Michigan? The salt, bromine, calcium, chloride, graphite, and brick regions?
7. Explain the etymological signification of "demonstration," "extraordinary," "accumulated," "Nova Scotia," "annually," "geological," "Arizona," "Montana," "advent."
8. How many words does Model I contain? II? III?
9. Discover and write out the framework of each model.
10. Find one subject on which you could make an item like Model I. Do the same for II and III.

VI. Written Composition

Remember that you are writing for the compositor. Every letter must be right. If you do a good piece of work it is altogether probable that your composition will get into one of the local papers.

VII. Suggested Reading

Mark Twain's *Tom Sawyer, Huckleberry Finn, Pudd'nhead Wilson,* or *Roughing It*.

VIII. Memorize

GOETHALS, THE PROPHET ENGINEER

A man went down to Panama
   Where many a man had died
To slit the sliding mountains
   And lift the eternal tide:
A man stood up in Panama,
   And the mountains stood aside.

For a poet wrought in Panama
   With a continent for his theme,
And he wrote with flood and fire
   To forge a planet's dream,
And the derricks rang his dithyrambs
   And his stanzas roared in steam.

[Page 28]
Where old Balboa bent his gaze
   He leads the liners through,
And the Horn that tossed Magellan
   Bellows a far halloo,
For where the navies never sailed
   Steamed Goethals and his crew;

CHAPTER VI
HUMOROUS ITEMS

"To laugh, if but for an instant only, has never been granted to man before the fortieth day from his birth."—PLINY.

I. Introduction

LAUGHTER, when it hurts nobody, is wholesome. It is the handmaid of happiness. It enriches life. Pleasant but not silly humor and wit are therefore altogether desirable in a paper. Few days in anybody's life are devoid of incidents that tickle the fancy. Material for good humorous stories is abundant everywhere. The faculty of recognizing it when it is seen, and the ability to present it effectively, however, need a little training. To make a beginning in these directions is the object of the exercises that follow.

II. Assignment

Find, but not in a book or a paper, a humorous story, and tell it, first orally, then in writing.

III. Models

I

Called on to decide the ownership of a hen claimed by George Bass and Joseph Nedrow, of Arnold City, Justice of the Peace John Reisinger hit upon a "Solomonesque" solution. "Take this fowl to Arnold City," he directed his constable, "and release it near the poultry yards of these two men. In whose hen house it goes to roost, to him it belongs." The constable, accompanied by Bass and Nedrow, did as directed. When liberated, the bird promptly flew into the chicken yard of Charles Black, where the constable decided it would have to stay under the justice's ruling. The costs in the case amount to ten times the value of the hen.

II

James M. I. Galloway, veterinary surgeon of Kirkintilloch, Scotland, arrived yesterday from Glasgow with photographs of a cow with a wooden leg on the starboard quarter, which the veterinary says is almost as good to the cow as an ordinary leg of beef and much more effective in knocking out folks who try to milk her on the wrong side.

Other veterinaries laughed at Galloway, who is young and of an experimental temperament, when he decided to save the life of this cow after the leg had been cut off by a locomotive. He insisted, however, on fitting the wooden leg, which he regards as much more useful than wooden heads on Scotch veterinaries.

The only time the wooden leg gets the cow into trouble is when she stands too long in a damp field and the leg sinks in a foot or so.

III

The written orders of Mr. J. W. Brooks, a once celebrated American railroad manager of Michigan, were, it is said, almost beyond deciphering. On a certain occasion, when a double track had been laid on one of his roads, it was reported at headquarters that the barn of an old farmer stood partly upon land which the company had bought, and dangerously near to passing trains. Mr. Brooks, who was just getting ready for a trip down the Mississippi, wrote to the farmer that he must move his barn from the company's land at once. If he delayed he would be liable to a suit for damages. The old farmer duly received the letter, and was able to make out the manager's signature, but not another word could he decipher. He took it to the village postmaster, who, equally unable to translate the hieroglyphics, was unwilling to acknowledge it. "Didn't you sell a strip of land to the railroad?" he asked. "Yes." "Well, I guess this is a free pass over the road." And for over a year the farmer used the manager's letter as a pass, not one of the conductors being able to dispute his translation of the instrument.

[Page 31] IV. Notes and Queries

1. A good story always has three parts: (1) A Situation; (2) a Climax; (3) a Solution. Do the models possess these elements? If they do, point them out.
2. Point out the "Four W's" in each.
3. Tell whether each sentence is simple, complex, or compound.
4. Tell why each mark of punctuation is used.
5. Tell why each capital letter is used.
6. Explain the syntax of the adjectives in I, the adverbs in II, the prepositions in III.
7. Explain the etymological signification of the following words: "solution"; "fowl"; "constable"; "photographs"; "veterinary"; "locomotive"; "decipher"; "liable"; "translate"; "hieroglyphics"; "conductors."
8. Find on the map Uniontown, Arnold City, Kirkintilloch, Michigan, and the Mississippi River.
9. Explain the reference in "Solomonesque."
10. What are "costs"?
11. Find a metaphor in II.

V. Suggested Time Schedule

As usual, except that on Friday one number of the program may be a magazine composed of the best stories written during the week by pupils.

VI. Oral Composition

Be sure that your story has a good point; is free from slang; and possesses a beginning, a middle, and an end.

VII. Written Composition

Suggestion: Imagine that the classroom is the local room of a daily paper, the pupils reporters, and the teacher the editor. The stories may be written in class.

VIII. Memorize

THE GRASSHOPPER AND THE CRICKET

The poetry of earth is never dead:
    When all the birds are faint with the hot sun,
    And hide in cooling trees, a voice will run
From hedge to hedge about the new-mown mead;
That is the Grasshopper's;—he takes the lead
    In summer luxury;—he has never done
    With his delights, for when tired out with fun
He rests at ease beneath some pleasant weed.
The poetry of earth is ceasing never:
    On a lone winter evening, when the frost
        Has wrought a silence, from the stove there shrills
The Cricket's song, in warmth increasing ever,
    And seems to one in drowsiness half lost
The Grasshopper's among some grassy hills.

                    JOHN KEATS.

CHAPTER VII
THE USE OF CONTRAST

"Give unto them beauty for ashes, the oil of joy for mourning, the garment of praise for the spirit of heaviness."—Isaiah.

I. Introduction

Antithesis, or contrast, is one of the two most effective devices at the disposal of any artist, whether he works with words or colors. Its skillful use often enables a newspaper writer to make a good item out of trifling material. The object of this week's work is to teach a little of the art of using antithesis effectively in reportorial work.

II. Models

I

London, Dec. 25.—Mrs. Rebecca Clarke, who is 109 years of age, presided this morning at the wedding breakfast of her baby son, Harry, who is 67. This is Mr. Clarke's second venture on the matrimonial sea. His two brothers are sprightly bachelors of 70 and 73 years. Mrs. Clarke toasted the newly married couple and ate the first slice of the wedding cake. She attended the Christmas wedding celebration in the evening.

II

Commuters in Yonkers took advantage of the Christmas holiday to mow their lawns. The grass has been getting longer and longer, owing to the spring weather, until it just had to be cut.

Players on the Dunwoodie Country Club course, also at Yonkers, had to keep moving to keep warm yesterday, but they played on greens which had been mowed only a few days ago, and those who were fond of flowers stopped now and then to pick a buttercup.

The greens keeper at Dunwoodie says that the greens have been mowed four times since the latter part of September, when in ordinary seasons the grass is mowed for the last time until spring. The condition of the course is about the same as in May, according to the greens keeper.

Up in Bronx Park the grass has not been mowed recently, but it is unusually long for the time of year, and so it is in the other city parks. The same condition prevails in the nearby cemeteries. Out in New Jersey a fine crop of grass is in evidence.

Farmers in the vicinity of New York are saving on their usual bills for winter fodder, for with the spring weather and the long grass the animals can pick up a living out of doors.

III

New York, Dec. 31.—An order for $2,000,000 worth of shrapnel, to be used in the war in Europe, has been rejected by the Commonwealth Steel Company of Granite City, Ill., it was learned to-day, because Clarence H. Howard, president of the organization, believes warfare should not be recognized.

Mr. Howard, who lives in St. Louis, is known all over the country as the "Golden rule steel man," because he tries to run his plant in accordance with the Golden Rule by sharing profits with the employes.

He is stopping at the Biltmore Hotel. Although he talked freely of the trouble in Europe, he frowned at the report about the $2,000,000 shrapnel order, and then said with blazing eyes:

"Why, our company would not accept an order for $15,000,000 worth of shrapnel! The war itself is a bitter shame. It is something that does not belong in the general scheme of enlightened humanity. If men would only think in unison, and think purely and strongly for the abolition of war, it would stop. There should be a general movement in the United States in this direction.

"When I was a youngster I left my home in Centralia, Ill., to win my own way in the world, and my mother gave [Page 35] me five maxims—one for each finger—which I since have followed with great profit. They are:

"'Seek company among those whom you can trust and association with whom will make you better.

"'Never gamble or go where gambling is done.

"'Never drink or go where drinking is done.

"'As to smoking, it isn't so bad as drinking or gambling, but take my advice and let it alone.

"'When in doubt about where to go, stop and ask if it would be a good place to take your mother.'

"Platitudes, eh! Some might call them that; but they have brought me happiness, and they have brought happiness to others. Not long ago I sat down and figured how much I had saved by not drinking, gambling, or the like. I figured it out at $1,000 a year, and it had been 30 years since my mother gave me the advice."

III. Notes

1. The contrast in Model I consists in the incongruity between the ages of the people and their occupations; in II the contrast is obviously the same as that alluded to in Byron's famous line,
      "Seek roses in December, ice in June";
   in III Mr. Howard's ideas, ideals, and conduct are in contrast with those of some men.
2. Antithesis between the actual and the normal is always interesting.

IV. Queries and Exercises

1. Explain the syntax of all nouns, adverbs, and infinitives in the models.
2. Find a metaphor in I.

3. Discuss the meaning and etymology of the following words: matrimonial, commuters, Christmas, December, animals.

4. Is "nearby" a better word than "adjacent"?

5. Where is Yonkers?

6. Tell whether the sentences are simple, compound, or complex.

7. [Page 36] What is the subject of each paragraph in II and III?

8. Write double headings for I and II. "Double" means in two parts. For example:

> **SHAKESPEARE CELEBRATION PLANS ADVANCE**
>
> President of Drama League Tells of Interest in Tercentenary Observances

Remember that you can use only a fixed number of letters in each line.

9. Define antithesis and metaphor. Find an example of each in to-day's paper.

V. Composition

1. *Choosing a Subject.* Select an incident that has come within the circle of your own observation; that has never, as far as you know, been described in print; and that is sufficiently unique to present a good contrast to the usual course of events.

2. *Collecting Material.* Get as many concrete details as possible. Generalities never glitter. They are useful only to cure insomnia.

3. *Arranging Material.* Look out for the "Four W's." Make a framework that is definite. It should be determined, in the last analysis, not by the model but by the material.

4. *Oral Composition.* Rehearse your article to your mother or to any other person whom you can induce to listen.
5. *Written Composition.* "Festinâ lente." "Hasten slowly." When a French student takes his college entrance examinations, he is plucked if he misspells one word, misplaces [Page 37] one capital letter, or makes a single mistake in punctuation. Lord Bacon somewhere says: "Let us proceed slowly that we may sooner make an end." Sheridan wrote:

> "You write with ease to show your breeding,
> But easy writing's curst hard reading."

Care in No. 5 will eliminate No. 6.
6. *Revision and rewriting.*

VI. Suggested Reading

Coleridge's *The Rime of the Ancient Mariner*.

VII. Memorize

MUSIC

Let me go where'er I will,
I hear a sky-born music still:
It sounds from all things old,
It sounds from all things young,
From all that's fair, from all that's foul,
Peals out a cheerful song.

It is not only in the rose,
It is not only in the bird,
Not only where the rainbow glows,
Nor in the song of woman heard,
But in the darkest, meanest things
There alway, alway something sings.

'Tis not in the high stars alone,
Nor in the cup of budding flowers,
Nor in the redbreast's mellow tone,

Nor in the bow that smiles in showers,
But in the mud and scum of things
There alway, alway something sings.
OLIVER WENDELL HOLMES.

TO TEACHERS. At this point a review of Chapter XII, "Vade Mecum, or Catechism," of *Practical English Composition,* Book I, will be found an invaluable exercise.

CHAPTER VIII
THRILLERS

> "'Tis strange, but true; for truth is always strange,
> Stranger than fiction."
>
> BYRON.

I. Assignments

1. RELATE the most exciting adventure that has occurred to you. Use the third person. Reporters usually are not allowed to use the pronoun "I."

2. Relate the most exciting adventure that has befallen any person whom you personally know well enough to interview on the subject.

3. If you can obtain material in neither of the foregoing ways, get a story from the movies, after the manner suggested in the following dispatch:

> TEACH REPORTING BY "MOVIES"
>
> *Journalism Instructors at Columbia Use Films to Develop Students' Faculty of Observation.*
>
> Reporters' "copy" telling in graphic style of the Balkan War poured into the "city room" of the newspaper plant at the Columbia University School of Journalism yesterday. The reason was that moving pictures had been adopted as a means of giving to the students an opportunity to exercise their powers of observation and description in such a fashion as would be required of them in real newspaper work.
>
> The idea of using a moving picture machine to train future newspaper reporters in accuracy of observation was originated by Professor Walter B. Pitkin, and was approved immediately by Dr. Talcott Williams, director of the school. Dr. C. E. Lower, instructor in English, is the official operator, but this work will probably be given later to a student.

4. A last resort is literature. In Stevenson, Poe, or Conan Doyle, you can probably find a story that can be translated into a sufficiently thrilling newspaper dispatch.

II. Models

I

Colonel Folque, commander of a division of artillery at the front, recently needed a few men for a perilous mission, and called for volunteers. "Those who undertake this mission will perhaps never come back," he said, "and he who commands will be one of the first sons of France to die for his country in this war."

Volunteers were numerous. A young graduate of a polytechnic school asked for the honor of leading those who would undertake the mission. It was the son of Colonel Folque. The latter paled, but did not flinch.

His son did not come back.—*Boston Herald.*

II

Villagers in fear of death were scuttling out of little homes like rats driven from holes by flood.

One person in the village remained at her accustomed post and from time to time recorded into the mouth of a telephone receiver the progress of the conflict, while a French general at the other end of the wire listened. Presently her communications were interrupted. "A bomb has just fallen in this office," the girl called to the general. Then conversation ceased.

It is always that way with the telephone girl when tragedy stalks abroad and there is necessity to maintain communication with the outside world. The telephone girl of Etain may be lionized in lyric literature. She deserves it. The telephone girl of Etain may find brief mention in history. She deserves that much at least. And yet the telephone girl at [Page 40] Etain is but one of her kind the world over.—*Sioux City Journal.*

III. Oral Composition

1. Point out in each story the situation, the climax, and the *dénouement*.
2. Discuss the meaning of "polytechnic," "lionized," "lyric."
3. Discuss the etymology of "volunteers," "mission," "graduate," "telephone," "literature."
4. Describe Etain.
5. Find in the models examples of antithesis, alliteration, and simile.

IV. Written Composition

1. Do not exceed the length of the models.
2. Be sure that your story is in three paragraphs, arranged thus: (1) Situation; (2) Climax; (3) Dénouement.
3. Put your story in the form of a news article with a heading. Don't forget the "Four W's."

V. Model

NEW YORK, November 21. The mystery of the disappearance of Mrs. Pauline Edwards on November 18 was cleared up to-day. A party of police visited her home at 96 East Twenty-third St. at 9 A.M. for the purpose of making a final examination of the premises. They found Mr. Allan Edwards, her husband, at home, and compelled him to accompany them on their tour of inspection. Careful scrutiny of all the rooms having failed to reveal any evidence of foul play, they were about to leave the cellar, which they had visited last, when Edwards, who was apparently under the influence of liquor or strong excitement, called their attention in abusive language to the construction of the walls, at the same time rapping heavily with a cane upon the bricks of the foundation of a chimney. His blows were answered by a sound from within the chimney. It seemed at first like the sobbing of a child and then swelled into an indescribable scream, howl, or shriek. The wall was broken down, revealing [Page 41] the bloody corpse of Mrs. Edwards. It stood erect. On its head sat a black cat.

On being arraigned before Police Justice O'Toole, Edwards confessed his guilt and told the story of his life. He comes from an excellent family, is a graduate of the University of Utopia, and had a thriving business until, several years ago, he became addicted to drink. During the summer of 1913, in a drunken frenzy, he gouged out one eye of a cat named Pluto, who had formerly been one of his pets. More recently he had destroyed this animal by hanging it with a clothes line in his yard. Remorse for this cruel deed caused him about two months ago to domesticate another cat, which was exactly like the first except that, whereas the first was entirely black, the second had on its breast a white spot, shaped like a gallows.

This circumstance, the fact that the animal had only one eye, and his own nervous condition soon made Edwards loathe and fear the new cat. On the morning of November 17, he and Mrs. Edwards went to the cellar to inspect their supply of coal. The cat followed them down the steep stairs and nearly overthrew Edwards, who thereupon seized an axe and would have slain it, had not Mrs. Edwards interposed. In his fury at being thwarted, he buried the axe in her skull. As the cellar had been newly plastered, he had no difficulty in removing some bricks from the chimney, in concealing the remains in its interior, and in repairing the wall in such a way that it did not differ in appearance from the rest of the cellar.

Dr. Felix Leo, Professor of Zoölogy at Columbia, on having these facts told him this morning, said he thought it unlikely that Cat Number Two was the same individual as Cat Number One, though the story of Androcles and the lion, if true, would indicate that animals of the feline species sometimes remember and reciprocate a kindness. "Why, then," said the doctor, solemnly closing one eye, "may we not suppose that a cat would have the will and the intelligence to revenge an injury?"

The theory of Edwards, who is now confined in a padded cell in the Tombs, is different. He maintains that the two cats are one and the same, and that the body of the beast is occupied by that ubiquitous spirit who is variously known as Satan, Hornie, Cloots, Mephistopheles, Pluto, and Old Nick.

VI. Analysis of Model

This story is simply a translation into newspaper English of Edgar Allen Poe's story entitled *The Black Cat*. Its three parts are as follows:

1. *Situation.* A man is converted by drink into such a beast that he first tortures and kills a pet and afterwards in his frenzy murders his wife, concealing her body in a chimney.
2. *Climax.* His crime is revealed by the wail of the cat, which he had supposed dead but had walled up with the corpse.
3. *Dénouement.* He is to be executed.

Poe puts the *dénouement* first, the situation second, and the climax last, which is a common and effective method in tales of horror and mystery. The newspaper method is to put the climax first, the *dénouement* second, and the situation last. This arrangement, which is as old as Homer's *Odyssey*, is thus alluded to by Byron:

> "Most epic poets plunge in *medias res*,
>   (Horace makes this the heroic turnpike road),
> And then your hero tells, whene'er you please,
>   What went before—by way of episode."

For newspaper purposes this method is desirable because it makes a good lead. That is, the first paragraph, and if possible the first sentence, tells the biggest fact about the case. Readers' attention being thus caught and economized, they get the habit of buying papers.

VII. Assignments

1. Write headlines for the models in this chapter.
2. Rewrite the Models in Section II on the plan of that in Section V.

3. Rewrite on the same plan one of Poe's other detective stories, one of Conan Doyle's Sherlock Holmes tales, Stevenson's *Dr. Jekyll and Mr. Hyde* or *The Wrecker*, one of Cooper's novels, or any other thrilling story.

[Page 43] VIII. Cautions

1. Be sure that you have your three situations in the right order.
2. Be exceedingly particular about the Four W's. Make them stand out vividly in each situation.
3. Use the shortest words that will convey your meaning.
4. Use adjectives and adverbs sparingly. How many does the model contain?

IX. Suggested Reading

Jules Verne's *Mysterious Island*; Robert Browning's *Hervé Riel*; Tennyson's *Revenge*; Whittier's *Barbara Frietchie*; Samuel Rogers's *Ginevra*.

X. Memorize

THE WAR-SONG OF DINAS VAWR

The mountain sheep are sweeter,
But the valley sheep are fatter;
We therefore deemed it meeter
To carry off the latter.
We made an expedition;
We met an host and quelled it;
We forced a strong position,
And killed the men who held it.

On Dyfed's richest valley,
Where herds of kine were browsing,
We made a mighty sally,
To furnish our carousing.
Fierce warriors rushed to meet us;
We met them, and o'erthrew them:
They struggled hard to beat us,
But we conquered them, and slew them.

As we drove our prize at leisure,
The king marched forth to catch us:
His rage surpassed all measure,
But his people could not match us.
He fled to his hall-pillars;
And, ere our force we led off,
Some sacked his house and cellars,
While others cut his head off.

We there, in strife bewildering,
Spilt blood enough to swim in:
We orphaned many children,
And widowed many women.
The eagles and the ravens
We glutted with our foemen;
The heroes and the cravens,
The spearmen and the bowmen.

We brought away from battle,
And much their land bemoaned them,
Two thousand head of cattle,
And the head of him who owned them:
Ednyfed, King of Dyfed,
His head was borne before us;
His wine and beasts supplied our feasts,
And his overthrow, our chorus.

     THOMAS LOVE PEACOCK.

CHAPTER IX
BOOK REVIEWS

"A good book is the precious life blood of a master spirit."

JOHN MILTON.

I. Assignments

    1. Write a review of a book of travels.

    2. Write a review of a biography.

    3. Write a review of a novel.

II. Models

I

FRASER, JOHN FOSTER. *The Amazing Argentine.* Pp. 291, illustrated. New York: Funk & Wagnalls Company. $1.50 net.

This volume should go far to dissipate any idea that there is not much of any consequence south of the Rio Grande besides the Panama Canal. In the story of his journeyings over the length and breadth of this enormous country—twice the size of Mexico—Mr. Fraser paints us a picture of a progressive people, and a country that is rapidly assuming a position as the foremost producer of the world's meat-supply. Stretching from the Atlantic to the Andes Mountains and from north of the Tropic of Capricorn to the Straits of Magellan, it supports 30,000,000 cattle, over 80,000,000 sheep, and 8,000,000 horses. The railroads, in which the British have invested £300,000,000, are among the best equipped in the world, and carry annually 40,000,000 tons of freight, with approximate receipts of £25,000,000. The export trade is advancing by leaps and bounds, and in 1912 the value of wool exports was £50,000,000, live-stock products £35,000,000, and agricultural produce £53,000,000; while the extent of the frozen-meat business may be gaged from the fact that £11,000,000 is invested in freezing-houses. [Page 46] The book is a distinct help to Americans in showing them a little more of the great country that is opening up to their enterprise.—*The Literary Digest,* October 17, 1914.2

II

LE SUEUR GORDON. *Cecil Rhodes.* 8vo, pp. 345. New York: McBride, Nast & Co. $3.50.

Cecil Rhodes must be looked upon as the Clive of South Africa. He found that country a land of wilderness and savagery. He transformed it into a fair and industrious province. He possessed the unscrupulous and relentless spirit of such conquerors as Julius Cæsar, and he was at the same time a financier of the widest resource. But some nefarious or alleged nefarious transactions which stained his name as a business man and a politician deprived him of royal recognition. He was not only denied a title, but even failed to obtain a decoration, and it was not until his death that a magnificent monument was unveiled to his memory in the heart of Rhodesia, a province which he had created and which was named after him.

Cecil John Rhodes (1853–1902) was born, like so many eminent Englishmen, in the house of a clergyman. Into the forty-nine years of his life he compressed a very stirring chapter of British victory. There was something of the buccaneer in his character when he prompted the notorious Jameson Raid and eventually brought the British Government into conflict with the cunning and ambition of Kruger—Oom Paul, as he was styled. For the bitter and bloody Boer War the blame has always been laid upon the shoulders of Rhodes.

Rhodes was an Oxford man and an omnivorous reader. He began by working in the diamond-mines at Kimberley as a common laborer; he ended by becoming manager of the Chartered Company, and amassing a vast fortune.—*The Literary Digest,* April, 1914.3

III

Sense and Sensibility. A Novel. By Jane Austen. London: Egerton. 1811.

Though inferior to *Pride and Prejudice,* this work is about as well worth reading as any novel which, previous to its publication, had been written in the English language. Its interest depends, not on its descriptive and narrative power, but on character portrayal and humor.

Though both lovable girls, the two heroines, Elinor and Marianne, are as imperfect and as different as sisters are apt to be in real life. Vulgar match-making Mrs. Jennings, as Austin Dobson calls her, like many a flesh-and-blood dowager, at first repels us by her foolish prattle and finally wins our respect by her kindness. Sir John Middleton, with his horror of being alone; Lady Middleton, with her horror of impropriety; Miss Steele, who can always be made happy by being teased about the Doctor; Lucy Steele, pretty, clever, not over-fastidious in her principles, and abominably weak in her grammar; Robert Ferrars, whose airs are justly punished by his marriage to Lucy; Mrs. Ferrars, who contrives to be uniformly unamiable; Mrs. John Dashwood, fit daughter to such a mother; and Mr. John Dashwood, fit husband to such a wife—together form a gallery of portraits of which any author might be proud.

The book, too, is rich in humor. Among other delightful things we read of a will which, like almost every other will, gave as much disappointment as pleasure; of a child of three who possesses the usual charms of that age, an imperfect articulation, an earnest desire of having his own way, many cunning tricks, and a great deal of noise; of apricot marmalade applied successfully as a remedy for a bruised temple; of a company who met to eat, drink, and laugh together, to play at cards or consequences, or any other game that was sufficiently noisy; of a husband who is always making remarks which his wife considers so droll but cannot remember; of Constantia wine, which is equally good for colicky gout and broken hearts; of a face of strong natural sterling insignificance; of a girl who was pleased that a man had called and still more pleased that she had missed him; of a woman of few words, for, unlike people in general, she proportioned [Page 48] them to the number of her ideas; of a newspaper item that interested nobody except those who knew its contents before; and of a man who was perfectly the gentleman in his behavior to guests and only occasionally rude to his wife and mother-in-law.

It is true that the two heroes are not very heroic, Edward Ferrars being only a curate and Col. Brandon a poor old man of 36 with a flannel waistcoat; but the latter is pretty thoroughly the gentleman and the former gives up a fortune of 30,000 pounds in order to marry a girl whom he does not love, thereby furnishing, if not an example of good sense, at least an agreeable contrast to Marianne's lover, Willoughby, who marries a girl whom he does not love in order to get the money which he is too genteel to earn.

On the whole, it is a wonderful book to have been written by a girl of twenty-one.4

III. Notes, Queries, and Exercises

1. Among the important functions of a newspaper is the task of announcing the appearance of new books, describing their contents, and commenting on their merits. The style of such notices should, above everything else, be clear. Most of them are unfortunately disfigured by a jargon which repels readers instead of inducing them to peruse the books reviewed.

2. What information should the heading of a book notice furnish?

3. Model I is an excellent example of what a review in a single paragraph should be. The first sentence bridges the intellectual and geographical space between the United States and Argentina, between the reader and the subject, which is just what an introduction should do. The second sentence describes the country in general terms, ending in a clause that leads directly to the most striking single fact about Argentina, its importance as an agricultural country. The three sentences that follow give concrete facts in support of this clause. The final sentence drives home the point stated in the first.

4. [Page 49] Discuss the meaning and etymology of "dissipate," "Rio Grande," "annually," "approximate," "exports," "enterprise."
5. Point out one restrictive and one non-restrictive clause.
6. Describe orally the location and character of the Rio Grande, Mexico, the Panama Canal, the Atlantic, the Andes, the Tropic of Capricorn, the British, and the Straits of Magellan.
7. What figure of speech have we in the phrase, "the Amazing Argentine?"
8. In Model II we have an illustration of a biographical review in three paragraphs. It presents a vivid picture of Cecil Rhodes in spite of the fact that it is not well organized. Try the experiment of rewriting it according to this plan: Par. I—Introduction, or Bridge; Par. II—Rhodes's Services to Mankind; Par. III—Rhodes's Faults; Par. IV—Rhodes's Private Life.
9. Find in the model an example of alliteration and an example of antithesis.
10. Explain the allusions in "Clive," "Julius Cæsar," "buccaneer," "Jameson Raid," "Kruger," "Boer War," and "Oxford."
11. Define "financier," "nefarious," "politician," "notorious," "ambition," and "omnivorous." From what language do these words come?
12. Analyze Model III as I and II have already been analyzed for you.
13. Find in III an antithesis and an alliteration.
14. Which of the books do you wish most to read? Why?
15. Do these models observe the law of presenting concrete rather than abstract statements?
16. Make a list of the books you have read, putting in one column the books of travel, into another the biographies, and into a third the novels.
17. Choose one of these as the subject of a review which you are to write.

IV. Oral Composition

In preparing for this observe the following points:

a. Remember that your main purpose is to persuade others to read the book.
b. [Page 50] In your first paragraph make a bridge from the minds of your audience to the book.

    c. In the body of your review describe concretely the one most interesting feature of the work.

    d. In your last paragraph restate the idea of the first but do it in some other form.

V. Written Composition

Concentrate your attention on perfection of sentence structure.

VI. Suggested Time Schedule

	Week I	Week II
Monday	Dictation	Oral Composition.
Tuesday	Dictation.	Oral Composition.
Wednesday	Notes, Queries, Exercises.	Written Composition.
Thursday	Notes, Queries, Exercises.	Revision.
Friday	Speaking.	Program.

VII. Suggested Reading

1. Macaulay's *Frederic the Great, Clive,* and *Hastings.*

2. Mark Twain's *Roughing It.*

3. Scott's *Ivanhoe.*

VIII. Memorize

    GUILIELMUS REX

    The folk who lived in Shakespeare's day
    And saw that gentle figure pass
    By London Bridge, his frequent way—
    They little knew what man he was.

    The pointed beard, the courteous mien,
    The equal port to high and low,
    All this they saw or might have seen—
    But not the light behind the brow!

The doublet's modest gray or brown,
The slender sword-hilt's plain device,
What sign had these for prince or clown?
Few turned, or none, to scan him twice.

Yet 'twas the king of England's kings!
The rest with all their pomps and trains
Are mouldered, half-remembered things—
'Tis he alone that lives and reigns!

THOMAS BAILEY ALDRICH.

[Page 52] CHAPTER X
REPORTING GAMES

> "It is not strength but art obtains the prize,
> And to be swift is less than to be wise."
>
> Iliad.

I. Assignment

If it is fall, report a football game; if winter, a basket-ball game; if spring or summer, a baseball game.

II. Material

In order to be able to report a football game, one must understand the rules of the game, be familiar with the *personnel* and history of the opposing teams, and know the names of the officials. The task therefore resolves itself into three parts:

1. Learning the rules of the game.
2. Studying the teams and officials.
3. Attending the game and taking notes.

Those members of the class who are familiar with the rules may be assigned the task of explaining them to the others; this is an excellent exercise in oral composition. It should include: (1) A short history of football; (2) A description of the field; (3) a description of the equipment of a team; (4) an account of the organization of a team; (5) a description of the way a game is played; (6) an explanation of the rules. *Spalding's Football Guide* contains all of the information necessary, though it may be supplemented by encyclopædias. It is suggested that this exercise be organized for presentation as a program.

[Page 53] The study of the opposing teams may be managed in the same way. It should include: (1) Their past history; (2) their *personnel*; (3) some account of the officials and their qualifications.

Quick and accurate observation of what happens during a game is essential. A good scheme for recording everything as it occurs is to make a chart of the field in a notebook, and, as the game progresses, to mark on it the progress of the ball, using a blue pencil when it is in the possession of one side and a red pencil when the other has it. On this chart brief notes of the methods by which the ball is advanced may also be made.

III. Composition

Football reports vary in length from a bare statement of the result of a game to many columns, the determining factor in this particular being the amount of public interest. The style is sometimes rendered picturesque by a skillful use of metaphor, antithesis, and slang, but more often is severely plain. The latter method is the only safe one for beginners. Except in the hands of a genius, the former is sure to result in silly vulgarity. The models which follow are of convenient length and in style are admirable, being clear, correct, and free from vulgarity.

IV. Models

I
MICHIGAN, 15; M.A.C., 3

Michigan defeated the Michigan Agricultural College at Lansing on Saturday, Oct. 14, in a game which marked the first defeat of the Aggies on their home field. The Wolverines went into the late minutes of the third quarter without [Page 54] a score and with 3 points against them, and, by the kind of football that has made Yost teams famous, played the "farmers" to a standstill. Michigan was returned a winner by a score of 15 to 3. The game brought out Jimmie Craig in the new rôle of halfback and assured him a permanent berth behind the line. Six hundred Michigan rooters attended the game.

The summary:

Michigan, 15	Position	*M.A.C.,* 3
Garrels	L.E.	Stone (Capt.) / Davis
Conklin (Capt.)	L.T.	Bekeman / Day
Bogle	L.G.	McLaughty
Paterson	C.	McWilliams

Michigan, 15	Position	M.A.C., 3
Allmendinger / Quinn	R.G.	Culver / Martin
Pontius	R.T.	Gifford
Wells	R.E.	Gorenflo
Craig / McMillan	Q.	Riblet
Torbet / Herrington / Craig	L.H.	Hill
Carpell	R.H.	Markem
Thomson	F.B.	Bullard / Julian

Officials—Referee, Hackett, West Point; Umpire, Eckersall, Chicago; Field Judge, Allen, Northwestern; Head Linesman, Yeckley, Penn. State. *Time of Periods*—10 minutes.

II
MICHIGAN, 19; OHIO STATE, 0

Michigan's defeat of O.S.U. on Ferry Field Saturday, October 21, was due largely to the superior endurance of the Wolverine team. State outplayed Michigan in the first quarter of the game, but Michigan soon settled to the task and rolled up 19 points against no score for the visitors. Foss, the Ohio quarterback, was the individual star of the game.

The summary:

Michigan, 19	Position	O.S.U., 0
Conklin (Capt.)	L.E.	Trautman / McCoy
Bogle / Roblee	L.T.	Barriklow
Bogle / Quinn	L.G.	Raymond
Paterson	C.	Geib
Allmendinger	R.G.	Geisman

Michigan, 19	Position	O.S.U., 0
Garrels } Pontius	R.T.	Markley (Capt.)
Wells	R.E.	{ Pavey / Stover
McMillan } Pickard	Q.	Foss
Craig	L.H.	Smith, L.J.
Carpell } Huebel	R.H.	Cox
Thomson	F.B.	{ Wright / Willaman

Officials—Referee, Thompson, Georgetown; Umpire, Hoagland, Princeton; Field Judge, Lieut. Nelly, West Point; Head Linesman, Macklin, Penn. *Time of periods*—15 minutes.

III
MICHIGAN, 9; VANDERBILT, 8

Michigan was played to a standstill in the game with McGugin's Vanderbilt eleven on Ferry Field Saturday, Oct. 28, and it was by the closest of margins that the Wolverines won out by a 9 to 8 score. A field goal was scored by each team and each team made a touchdown, but Michigan was more fortunate than her southern rivals in that McMillan made a perfect punt-out and Conklin kicked goal, while Captain Roy Morrison of Vanderbilt fell down on the same play and lost his team the chance to try for a goal from touchdown when he overkicked on the punt-out. Yost was far from satisfied by the showing of the Michigan team.

The summary:

Michigan, 9	Position	Vanderbilt, 8
Conklin (Capt.)	L.E.	K. Morrison
Bogle	L.T.	{ Freeland / Covington

Michigan, 9	Position	Vanderbilt, 8
Quinn	L.G.	Metzger
Paterson	C.	Morgan
Garrels	R.G.	C. Brown
Pontius	R.T.	T. Brown
Wells	R.E.	E. Brown
McMillan	Q.	R. Morrison (Capt.)
Craig	L.H.	Hardage
Carpel	R.H.	{ Collins / Curlin
Thomson	F.B.	Sikes

Officials—Referee, Bradley Walker, Virginia; Umpire, Eckersall, Chicago; Field Judge, Lieut. Nelly, West Point; Head Linesman, Heston, Michigan.

G. E. ELDERIDGE.
Michigan Alumnus, November, 1911.

V. Queries and Topics for Oral Composition

1. What knowledge is necessary in order to report a football game?
2. How old is the game of football?
3. Wherein do Rugby, soccer, Canadian, and American football differ?
4. Describe the field on which American football is played.
5. Describe the shoes, costumes, headgear, and ball used in the game.
6. What is a stadium?
7. Describe the functions of each player on a team.
8. Explain the following terms: "kickoff," "tackling," "end run," "line buck," "interference," "blocking," "holding," "off side," "punt," "drop kick," "forward pass," "fair catch," "downs," "scrimmage," "touchdown," "touchback," "safety," "goal from touchdown," and "goal from field."
9. How many yards must a team carry the ball in four downs in order to keep it?
10. How much does a touchdown count? A safety? A field goal? A goal from touchdown?

11. [Page 57] How would you go to work to find out the past history of a team and the character of its personnel?
12. What method of taking notes is recommended?
13. How long should the report of a game be?
14. In what style should it be written?
15. How many words does each model contain?
16. Observe how the writer seizes on the one or two salient points of each game, omitting what is unessential. This requires judgment and the effort to do it is a good training in judgment.
17. Tell whether each sentence is simple, complex, or compound.
18. Explain why each mark of punctuation is used.
19. Find a metaphor in the models.

VI. Exercise

Write a report of Saturday's game.

VII. Suggested Time Schedule

	Week I	*Week II*
Monday—	(a) Review past errors. (b) Assign work on Sections II and III of this chapter.	Queries.
Tuesday—	Program on Section II.	Queries.
Wednesday—	Program on Section III.	Oral Composition
Thursday—	Dictation of Models.	Written Composition and Reviews.
Friday—	Dictation of Models.	Public Speaking.

VIII. Suggested Reading

Thomas Hughes's *Tom Brown at Rugby*; Homer's *Iliad,* Book XXIII; Virgil's *Æneid,* Book v.

IX. Model II.

NEW YORK, October 9, 1913.—Cornelius McGillicuddy's Murder Association, incorporated, convened at the Polo grounds this afternoon, transacted routine business, and adjourned.

On motion of Brother Edward Collins, supported by [Page 58] Brother J. Franklin Baker, and carried by acclamation, it was voted to resume the task of tearing the hide off the Giants. Messrs. Collins and Baker were appointed a special committee of two to carry out the work and seven others were assigned to assist them.

After the meeting refreshments consisting of singles, doubles, triples, and home runs were served; and a good time was had by all, excepting John J. McGraw and his employes and friends numbering upward of 25,000. The latter class was unanimous in declaring the Mackmen a bunch of vulgar, common persons who play professional baseball for a living and thus are not entitled to associate with amateurs, such as some of the New York players.

To get to the point of things, Philadelphia had what some of the fans called "one of them afternoons." There is no use trying to describe all the details of this so-called contest, for it is demoralizing to the young to see such things in print. Many criminals have confessed on the scaffold that they got their start watching the Athletics assault some honest young pitcher who was trying to support his aged mother. They say that, if the Macks can get away with their rough work, anything ought to go.

Eight to two was the score to-day, if anybody cares. We can't just figure out where New York got the two, but it was there on the score board and must have happened. Also there is a well-grounded belief that McGraw has subsidized the scoreboard boy so that he cheats the visitors somewhat. But, anyhow, it is reasonably certain that the Mackmen had plenty, while New

York was several shy of the total that would have cheered the heart of Gotham, if indeed Gotham has a heart.

Connie Mack and John J. McGraw each had to do some guessing to-day in the matter of picking a pitcher. Lean Connie picked up the right answer and Fat John did not. There's the whole story. The Philadelphia boss shook up the names of his young pitchers in a hat, shut his eyes, and drew out the name of Joe Bush. McGraw, by and with the consent and advice of his entire club, picked Jeff Tesreau. At least it was popularly believed, during and before the game started, that John had given his mound corps a careful slant and chosen Jeff as the best bet. Afterward some of the [Page 59] experts believed that the New York manager, by way of showing a delicate bit of courtesy to a guest, had accorded Connie the privilege of naming New York's gunner. Certainly Tesreau was the best player Philadelphia had and the Athletics were seriously crippled when he retired in the seventh, just after Baker had knocked Doyle's right leg out into the field.

About all that Tesreau had was a fine physique and a mouthful of slippery elm. Almost before the umpires and managers had ceased to chat over the rules, the Macks had lumped three hits, and with a wild heave by Artie Fletcher had scored three runs, which was one more than the Giants got all day. In the next inning some more hammering gave another pair of markers. Then Tesreau settled down and went along fairly well until the seventh. The Athletics had another rush of hits to the outfield in this inning and Otis Crandall came in to finish up the contest, or scandal, whichever you choose to term it. By this time Connie's men were getting hungry for supper, so they made only one tally off Crandall, this coming when Wallie Schang bakered one into the right field stand.

Of course, under such conditions, Joe Bush didn't have a real test. Connie Mack himself, or his crippled batboy, could have pitched the game and won it from the second inning on. Joe just kept slamming them over and, though he had a couple of wild spells that gave the Giants a chance to figure in the game, he always was able to pull himself together before there was any real danger.

Nobody here had heard much about this Joe Bush previous to to-day. Even the experts, who see all things that are and a lot that aren't, didn't have the dope on him. They had heard of Donie Bush and Anheuser Busch and Bush leaguers, but Joseph was a new one. For the information and guidance of those who may be interested, we furnish the data that he came From the Missoula Club of the Union—or is it Onion—Association last fall, and is a right hander.

Bush has the reputation of being almost as speedy as Walter Johnson on his good days and this was one of them. In the early stages of the game he depended almost entirely on his fast ball but later began to unbelt a few curves which had the right sort of a fold to them. Although in a hole with [Page 60] many batters, he passed only four and hit one. Great fielding helped him at times, the Macks pulling off a double play in each of three innings in which New York appeared to have something started.

Any child wonder who can come all the way from Missoula to Broadway in one year and win a world's series game is of course entitled to much credit, but this boy certainly fell into a particularly soft spot. With the Macks' billion dollar infield killing base hits for him and the attack getting him eight runs, he would have had a hard time slipping the game to McGraw if he had sold out before hostilities started. Bush permitted the Giants, who were commonly reported to be moaning for the gore of Mack's youngsters, just five hits. Two of these were bunched in one inning and resulted in one of the runs. The others straggled through.[5]

The Score

PHILADELPHIA	AB	R	H	TB	BB	SH	SB	PO	A	E
E. Murphy, r.f.	5	1	2	2	0	0	0	2	0	0
Oldring, l.f.	5	3	2	2	0	0	1	0	0	0
Collins, 2b.	5	2	3	5	0	0	1	5	4	0

PHILADELPHIA	AB	R	H	TB	BB	SH	SB	PO	A	E
Baker, 3b.	4	1	2	2	0	0	1	3	1	0
McInnis, 1b.	4	0	0	0	0	0	0	9	0	0
Strunk, c.f.	4	0	0	0	0	0	0	1	0	0
Barry, s.s.	4	0	1	1	0	0	0	2	3	0
Schang, c.	4	1	1	4	0	0	0	5	2	1
Bush, p.	4	0	1	1	0	0	0	0	1	0
Total	39	8	12	17	0	0	3	27	11	1

NEW YORK	AB	R	H	TB	BB	SH	SB	PO	A	E
Herzog, 3b.	4	0	0	0	0	0	0	1	0	0
Doyle, 2b.	4	0	1	1	0	0	0	5	1	0
Fletcher, s.s.	2	0	1	1	1	0	1	2	2	1
Burns, l.f.	4	0	0	0	0	0	0	3	0	0
Shafer, c.f.	3	1	1	2	1	0	0	2	0	0
Murray, r.f.	3	1	1	1	1	0	1	4	0	0
McLean, c.	2	0	1	1	0	0	0	3	1	0
Wilson, c.	2	0	0	0	0	0	0	2	0	0
Merkle, 1b.	2	0	0	0	1	0	0	3	0	0
Wiltse, 1b.	0	0	0	0	0	0	0	2	0	0
Tesreau, p.	2	0	0	0	0	0	0	0	0	0
Crandall, p.	1	0	0	0	0	0	0	0	2	0
*Cooper	0	0	0	0	0	0	1	0	0	0
Total	29	2	5	6	4	0	3	27	6	1

| Philadelphia | 3 | 2 | 0 | 0 | 0 | 0 | 2 | 1 | 0—8 |
| New York | 0 | 0 | 0 | 0 | 1 | 0 | 1 | 0 | 0—2 |

* Ran for McLean in fifth.

Two-base hit—Shafer. Three-base hit—Collins. Home run—Schang. Struck out—by Tesreau, 3; by Crandall, 1; by Bush, 3. Double plays—Collins-Barry; Bush-Barry-McInnis; Doyle (unassisted); Schang-Collins. Time—2:11. Umpires—Rigler at plate, Connolly on bases, Klem and Egan in field.

X. Exercises

1. In this report we have a good example of baseball reporting as a literary art. The writer, Mr. E. A. Batchelor, of the *Detroit Free Press*, uses metaphor and antithesis with effect. The framework, as is usual in good comic writing, is excellent. Observe it:

    1. Four W's—Par. 1.
    2. Business Meeting—Par. 2.
    3. Refreshments—Pars. 3–12, inclusive.

        What New York suffered—Par. 3.

        What Philadelphia did—Par. 4.

        The Score—Par. 5.

        The Pitchers—Pars. 6–10.

        > Their Choice—Par. 6.
        >
        > What New York's didn't do—Pars. 7–8.
        >
        > Joe Bush—Pars. 9–12.

2. *Use of Metaphor.* (*a*) Analyze the metaphor in "Murder Association." (*b*) Point out the words in the first three paragraphs that serve to sustain and amplify the comparison. (*c*) Explain the metaphors that lurk in "rush of hits to the outfield," "bakered," "unbelt," "in a hole," "straggled through."

3. *Antithesis.* In Par. 3 the first sentence contains a fine contrast, "A good time was had by all, excepting," etc., "all" including fewer persons than there are in the group excepted. It is an old but good trick. In the same paragraph note also the contrast between professionals and amateurs. The rest of the story contains at least a half-dozen antitheses in addition to those already mentioned. Find them.

4. *Topics for short expository speeches*: Cornelius McGillicuddy; J. Franklin Baker; the Giants; John J. McGraw; The Spelling of the Word "Athletics"; How Baseball is Played; Gotham; Joe Bush; Jeff Tesreau; Doyle; A Mouthful of Slippery Elm; Otis Crandall; Wallie Schang; Donie Bush; Missoula; Curves; Broadway; The Macks' Billion Dollar Infield.

5. *Translate*: "The fans"; "one of them afternoons"; "if the Macks can get away with their rough work, anything ought to go"; "shy"; "a careful slant"; "his best bet"; "slamming them over"; "pulling off a double play"; [Page 62] "something started"; "slipping the game to McGraw."

6. *Subject for Debate*: Resolved—that the use of slang should be avoided.

7. Make a study of the art of reporting baseball games, following the hints for football already given, and report a school game. The boys in the class can be relied upon to furnish all of the technical information that will be needed.

XI. Memorize

ENDYMION

A thing of beauty is a joy for ever:
Its loveliness increases; it will never
Pass into nothingness; but still will keep
A bower quiet for us, and a sleep
Full of sweet dreams, and health, and quiet breathing.
Therefore, on every morrow, we are wreathing
A flowery band to bind us to the earth,
Spite of despondence, of the inhuman dearth
Of noble natures, of the gloomy days,
Of all the unhealthy and o'er-darkened ways
Made for our searching: yes, in spite of all,

Some shape of beauty moves away the pall
From our dark spirits. Such the sun, the moon,
Trees old and young, sprouting a shady boon
For simple sheep; and such are daffodils
With the green world they live in; and clear rills
That for themselves a cooling covert make
'Gainst the hot season; the mid forest brake,
Rich with a sprinkling of fair musk-rose blooms:
And such too is the grandeur of the dooms
We have imagined for the mighty dead;
All lovely tales that we have heard or read:
An endless fountain of immortal drink,
Pouring unto us from the heaven's brink.

JOHN KEATS.

CHAPTER XI
REPORTING SPEECHES

> "Words are like leaves, and where they most abound
> Much fruit of sense beneath is seldom found."
>
> POPE.

I. Assignment

REPORT a speech, lecture, or sermon in two hundred words.

II. Explanation

It is easy to obtain the material for this assignment because one has only to attend, listen, and take notes. Indeed, in some instances, speakers are ready and willing to furnish reporters with copies of what they intend to say. The part of the task which requires skill is what is known as boiling down, condensing, or reducing the report to the dimensions required by editors. This involves: first and foremost, a determination not to misrepresent in any way what is said; second, the ability to select the essential points; third, an eye for such detail as may be used to spice the report without making it too long. Too many reporters, in their anxiety to make a good story, observe only the last of these requirements, and in consequence are unjust to speakers. In the arrangement of the material, it is well to begin with a statement of the main point of the speech and to follow it with such details as space permits.

III. Speech Construction

Every good speech, however long, has only one main point. Its details serve only to illustrate and enforce this central theme. The reporter needs to bear this in mind. He must discover the central point, or thesis, before he can write a good report. A knowledge of the principles underlying speech construction is therefore of great value to him, even if not essential. Fortunately, these are comparatively simple. Nearly every good speech, from Demosthenes down, has consisted of the following parts in the following order:

1. *Exordium, or Introduction.* A bridge from the audience to the subject, designed to conciliate and interest.
2. *Status, or Plan.* An outline of what the speaker intends to say.
3. *Statement of Facts.* A presentation of the situation on which the orator intends to found his argument.
4. *Argument.* Here is presented in detail the plan or conclusion which the speaker has in mind, with the reasons in favor of it.
5. *Refutation.* A reply to objections which have been or may be urged against the plan.
6. *Peroration, or Conclusion.* This may be a summary of the speech, a good-humored bit of color, a picture of the benefits to be derived from the adoption of the orator's plan, or an impassioned appeal for action.

Sermons and political speeches are usually argumentative and hence of this type. Sometimes, however, an orator and his theme are so well known that he omits all except 3 and 4; occasionally all except 4 disappear. Lectures often contain only 3, as their purpose is only to convey information. Usually, however, a speech without an argument is like a gas engine without gas; it has no "go." The speech that [Page 65] does not aim to get people to do something is usually flat, stale, and unprofitable.

IV. Models

I

LONDON, March 22, 1775.—Conciliation as a means of allaying the present discontent in the American colonies was advocated in the House of Commons to-day by Mr. Edmund Burke. He proposed that Parliament abandon the idea of taxing the colonies, and instead place on the statute book an act acknowledging that the various colonial legislative bodies have the power to grant or refuse aids to the crown. Though his speech, which lasted over three hours, was heard with respect, the measures which he proposed were defeated by a strict party vote, 270 to 78.

Mr. Burke spoke with a dignity and power which have not been surpassed even by the Earl of Chatham. His mastery of the subject was so complete and the form of his speech so perfect that competent judges pronounce it a classic. His speech is to be printed at once as a pamphlet.

In outline Mr. Burke said: "As I have studied this American question for years, have held fixed opinions on it since 1766, and have nothing to gain except disgrace if I suggest a foolish solution of the problem, I believe that you will hear me with patience. My speech will consist of the discussion of two questions: (1) Should we attempt to conciliate the Americans? (2) If so, how? America is already powerful by virtue of population, commerce, and agriculture. The chief characteristic of the American people is their fierce love of freedom. There are only three ways to deal with this spirit: (1) To remove it by removing its causes; (2) to punish it as criminal; (3) to comply with it as necessary. Its causes are irremovable, being the love of independence which caused their ancestors to leave England; their religion in the North, which is the Protestantism of the Protestant religion; the fact that in the South they hold slaves; the general diffusion among them of education; the circumstance that they speak English and that an Englishman is the unfittest man on earth to argue another Englishman into being a slave; and [Page 66] the 3000 miles of ocean, between us and them. It cannot be treated as criminal, there being no way to draw up an indictment against a whole nation. Indeed, you have already tried to do this and failed. There remains no way of treating the American spirit except to comply with it as necessary. I propose, therefore, to erect a Temple of British Concord with six massive pillars by granting to America in six propositions the identical rights which for generations have been by acts of Parliament secured to Ireland, Wales, Chester, and Durham, except that, owing to the distance of America from England, each colony, instead of sending members to Parliament, shall have the power, through its own legislature, to grant or refuse aids to the Crown. If adopted, these measures, I believe, will substitute an immediate and lasting peace for the disorders which Lord North's measures have created. The unbought loyalty of a free people, thus secured, will give us more revenue than any coercive measure. Indeed, it is the only cement that can hold together the British Empire."

II

EDINBURGH, Sept. 20, 1887.—Edmund Burke was the theme of a lecture delivered last night before the Edinburgh Philosophical Society by Mr. Augustine Birrell. "Nobody is fit to govern this country who has not drunk deep at the springs of Burke," said Mr. Birrell, and he backed up this contention with a wealth of wit and argument which delighted and convinced his audience.

The following is a summary of his lecture: "To give a full account of Burke's public life is no part of my plan. I propose merely to sketch his early career, to explain why he never obtained a seat in the cabinet, and to essay an analysis of the essential elements of his greatness. Born in 1729 in Dublin, he grew up with a brother who speculated and a sister of a type who never did any man any serious harm; acquired at school a brogue which death alone could silence; at Trinity College, Dublin, became an omnivorous reader; came in 1750 to London to study law, armed with a cultivated curiosity and no desperate determination to make his fortune; immediately, like the sensible Irishman he was, fell [Page 67] in love with Peg Woffington; for six years rambled everywhere his purse permitted, read everything he could lay his hands on, and talked everlastingly; in 1756 published an 'Essay on the Sublime and Beautiful,' and married Miss Jane Mary Nugent; in 1758 dared at David Garrick's dinner table to contradict Dr. Johnson; in 1765 became a member of Parliament; and for the next sixteen years was the life and soul of the Whig party. When that party, in 1782, finally came into power, Burke's only reward, however, was a minor office, a fact which, in view of his great merits, has amazed posterity. The explanation is that his contemporaries probably knew him, not as a commanding genius, but as an Irishman who was always in debt, whose relatives were rather disreputable, whose judgment was often wrong, and whose temper was violent. His significance for us grows from the fact that he applied the imagination of a poet of the first order to the business of life. He saw organized society steadily and saw it whole. Perceiving that only a thin crust of conventionality protects organized society from the volcanic heats of anarchy, he was afraid of reformers. He could not agree to dispense with the protection afforded by the huge mountains of prejudice and the ancient rivers of custom. He was the High Priest of Order. He loved justice and hated iniquity. The world needs his wisdom to-day."

Mr. Birrell's lecture was full of good phrases. For instance:

1. We have the spectacle of Burke in his old age, like another Laocoön, writhing and wrestling with the French Revolution.
2. Lubricating religious differences with the sweet oil of the domestic affections.
3. Quaint old landladies wonder maternally why he never gets drunk, and generally mistake him for an author until he pays his bill.
4. I love him for letting me warm my hands at it (his wrath at Gerard Hamilton) after a lapse of a hundred and twenty years.
5. His letters to Arthur Young on the subject of carrots still tremble with emotion.
6. This is magnificent, but it is not farming.

V. Queries

1. What part of the task of reporting a speech is easy? Why?
2. Wherein lies its difficulty?
3. What are the three essentials of a good report?
4. What is the commonest fault in reporting speeches?

5. What arrangement of material is suggested?
6. How many main ideas should a speech contain?
7. Name and describe the six parts of a speech.
8. Are any of them ever omitted? When, how, and by whom?
9. Discuss the value of argument in a lecture.
10. Who was Demosthenes?
11. When did the battle of Lexington occur?
12. Discuss the etymology of "Parliament."
13. Explain the subject of each paragraph in Model I.
14. Divide Paragraph 3, Model I, into the six parts of a complete speech.
15. What are the important places in a sentence? Did the writer of these models recognize this fact?
16. Find a metaphor in Model I. An alliteration. An antithesis.
17. Point out the Four W's, and discuss the sentence structure.
18. What is the subject of each paragraph in Model II?
19. Write a note of fifty words on Augustine Birrell.
20. Explain the nature and location of Ireland, Wales, Chester, Durham, Dublin, Edinburgh, London.
21. Who were David Garrick and Dr. Johnson?
22. Why did Burke stand no higher with his contemporaries?
23. Explain the nature of Burke's importance to the world to-day.
24. Have the British adopted his principles in the management of Canada, Australia, New Zealand, and South Africa?
25. Explain the figure of speech in each quotation in the last paragraph of Model II.
26. Find in Paragraph 2 of Model II a metaphor and an antithesis.
27. How many of the six parts of a speech can you find in Lincoln's Gettysburg speech?

[Page 69] **VI. Composition**

Hear and report a speech. If this appears to be undesirable or impossible, the teacher may read one to the class. The following are suggested:

1. Macaulay's *Speech on Education*.
2. One of the lectures in Thackeray's *English Humorists* or *Four Georges*.
3. Phillips's *Toussaint L'Ouverture*.
4. Webster's *Bunker Hill Speeches*.
5. Lincoln's *Peoria Speech* against Douglas.
6. One of Birrell's *Obiter Dicta Lectures*.

Others equally good will probably suggest themselves.

VII. Suggested Time Schedule[6]

	Week I	*Week II*
Monday—	I, II, III.	V, 15–27.
Tuesday—	IV, 1.	Oral Composition.
Wednesday—	IV, 2.	Oral Composition.
Thursday—	V, 1–14.	Written Composition.
Friday—	Speaking.	Speaking.

[Page 70] **VIII. Memorize**

THE DESTRUCTION OF SENNACHERIB

The Assyrian came down like the wolf on the fold,
And his cohorts were gleaming in purple and gold;
And the sheen of their spears was like stars on the sea,
When the blue wave rolls nightly on deep Galilee.

Like the leaves of the forest when Summer is green,

That host with their banners at sunset were seen;
Like the leaves of the forest when Autumn hath blown,
That host on the morrow lay withered and strown.

For the Angel of Death spread his wings on the blast
And breathed in the face of the foe as he passed;
And the eyes of the sleepers waxed deadly and chill,
And their hearts but once heaved and forever grew still!

. . . .

And the widows of Ashur are loud in their wail,
And the idols are broke in the temple of Baal;
And the might of the Gentiles, unsmote by the sword,
Hath melted like snow in the glance of the Lord.
                    LORD BYRON.

CHAPTER XII
DRAMATIC NOTICES

"To hold the mirror up to Nature."

SHAKESPEARE.

I. Assignment

WRITE a notice of one of the plays now on the local stage.

II. Explanation

To keep its readers informed of the character of the plays being presented at local theaters is one of the functions of the newspaper. If the play is a classic, only the quality of the acting need be discussed. If it is new, the notice should also include a description of the play and of its merit. Fortunately, this can always be determined by one simple test—a test suggested by no less a critic than William Shakespeare: Does it hold the mirror up to nature? Does it give, in other words, an accurate picture of life? The stage, it may be added, always has been and is now infested by many so-called plays which are not plays at all, but mere conglomerations of more or less (usually less) moral and amusing jokes and antics. The events which some of them depict could occur neither on the earth, in the sky above the earth, nor in the waters underneath the earth. From others it would be impossible to cut out any character or scene without improving the whole. They fill the theater with people and the manager's pocket-book with money, but they are not plays.

III. Models

I

The Melting Pot comes to New York with a Chicago indorsement and the authority lent by the name of Mr. Israel Zangwill, as author. Mr. Zangwill's theme is that the United States is a crucible in which all the races and nationalities of the world are to be fused into one glorious people.

As a play *The Melting Pot* has the intellectual tone to be expected from Mr. Zangwill. It also has really poetic touches. In humor it is less successful. In dramatic construction it is faulty, as are so many of the contemporary plays which try to teach or preach something.

The play brings back to New York after a long absence that excellent actor, Mr. Walker Whiteside.—METCALFE in *Life* (abbreviated).[7]

II

Of *David Copperfield*, Dickens's favorite among his own works, there have been dramatizations almost innumerable. The latest, called the *Highway of Life*, by Louis N. Parker, author of *Pomander Walk* and *Disraeli*, has been done with extreme reverence for the text and with an elaborate scenic investiture that would have made glad the heart of the novelist, enamored as he was of the theater.

It was to have been the autumn offering at His Majesty's in London, with Sir Herbert Tree doubling as *Micawber* and *Dan'l Peggotty*. The war caused a change of plans, so the first performance on any stage took place at Wallack's in New York. Lennox Pawle, Mr. Parker's son-in-law, realized a long-cherished ambition to step forth as *Micawber*. Fresh from his multimillionaire of *The Money Makers*, came Emmet Corrigan for *Dan'l Peggotty*. *Betsey Trotwood* fell to Eva Vincent. The Lieblers were especially happy in their selection of a *Mrs. Micawber* in the person of Maggie Holloway Fisher. She spent days digging out and fashioning the costume she wears, and no one ever murdered a song more successfully than she at David's dinner-party. An astonishingly faithful imitation of her languishing airs is given by Philip [Page 73] Tonge, when, as *Traddles*, he reads *Micawber's* letter. J. V. Bryant, the *Copperfield*, and Vernon Steele, the *Steerforth*, are both English. O. P. Heggie deserves more than a passing word of commendation for the things he refrains from doing as *Uriah Heep*. He is not forever going through that waterless washing of the hands.

There are ten different sets of scenery in *The Highway of Life*, all charming or effective as the case may be. For the background of Mr. Wickfield's garden at Canterbury we have a glimpse of the famous cathedral, and from *Betsey Trotwood's* domain we get a view of the chalk cliffs and downs at Dover. A happy conceit throws shadow pictures of the principal characters upon a sheet as they cross the stage just before the first curtain rises.
—MATTHEW WHITE, JR., in *Munsey's* (abbreviated).[8]

IV. Notes and Queries

1. What is the subject of each paragraph in Model I?
2. Explain the function of each sentence in Model I.
3. Discuss the meaning and etymology of the following terms: Chicago indorsement; theme; crucible; fuse; contemporary.
4. Who is Israel Zangwill?

5. Tell the story of David Copperfield.
6. Why does Matthew White not tell it?
7. Discuss the uses of the apostrophe.
8. Discuss the meaning and etymology of: dramatization; extreme; elaborate; investiture; novelist; enamored; theater; doubling; ambition; sets.
9. What is the subject of each paragraph in Model II?
10. Find at least two metaphors in the models.

V. Gathering Material

Material for this exercise may be secured in three places:

1. At the theater.
2. [Page 74] At a school play.
3. By reading, in case there is no chance to see a play, one of the following:

    Fitch, W. C. *Barbara Frietchie*, or *Nathan Hale*.
    Gilbert, W. S. *The Mikado*, or *Pinafore*.
    Goldsmith, O. *She Stoops to Conquer*.
    Maeterlinck, Maurice. *The Bluebird*.
    Phillips, Stephen. *Ulysses*.
    Shakespeare, W. Any play.
    Shaw, G. B. *Cæsar and Cleopatra*.
    Sheridan, R. B. *The Rivals*, or *The School for Scandal*.
    Tarkington, Booth. *The Man from Home*.

VI. Organization

From the following list of paragraph topics, select those which are best worth discussing in connection with the play which you desire to review. Select those about which you can get the fullest information.

1. The Four W's.
2. The Story.
3. The Theme.
4. Poetry.
5. Humor.
6. Construction.
7. Philosophy.
8. The Actors.
9. The Scenery.
10. Character Portrayal.

If the play is noteworthy for its poetry, its wit, or its philosophy, these should be illustrated by one or two quotations. If the chief interest is in the story, tell the story. If its strength is derived from the skill of the actors, from the setting, or from character portrayal, devote your attention to a clear exposition of these phases of the play. Do not permit your notice to be shorter than I nor longer than II.

VII. Suggested Time Schedule

Monday—Discussion of Mistakes in former Themes.
Tuesday—Study of Models through Dictation.
Wednesday—Gathering of Material—Organization.
Thursday—Oral Discussion of First Drafts.
Friday—1. Present finished work to teacher.
        2. Program.

VIII. A Shakespeare Program

If, for any reason, it seems unwise to send pupils to a play, they might be requested (1) to present the following program, or some modification of it, as typical of Shakespeare's best work, and (2) to write notices or critiques thereon. It is perhaps unnecessary to add that no more profitable or delightful exercise can be devised for a class.

1. Mendelssohn's *A Midsummer Night's Dream* Music.
2. Antony's Oration (with mob).
3. Songs from *As You Like It*.
4. Quarrel of Brutus and Cassius.
5. The Seven Ages of Man.
6. Hamlet's Soliloquy.
7. The Trial Scene from *The Merchant of Venice*.
8. Songs from Various Plays.
9. The Rude Mechanicals, from *A Midsummer Night's Dream*.

IX. Memorize

THE ART OF ACTING

Hamlet. Speak the speech, I pray you, as I pronounced it to you, trippingly on the tongue: but, if you mouth it, as many of your players do, I had as lief the town-crier spoke my lines. Nor do not saw the air too much with your hand, thus, but use all gently; for in the very torrent, tempest, and, as I may say, the whirlwind of passion, you must acquire and beget a temperance that may give it smoothness. O, it offends me to the soul to hear a robustious periwig-pated [Page 76] fellow tear a passion to tatters, to very rags, to split the ears of the groundlings, who for the most part are capable of nothing but inexplicable dumb-shows and noise: I would have such a fellow whipped for o'erdoing Termagant; it out-herods Herod: pray you, avoid it.

First Player. I warrant your honour.

Hamlet. Be not too tame neither, but let your own discretion be your tutor: suit the action to the word, the word to the action; with this special observance, that you o'erstep not the modesty of nature: for anything so overdone is from the purpose of playing, whose end, both at the first and now, was and is, to hold, as 'twere, the mirror up to nature; to show virtue her own feature, scorn her own image, and the very age and body of the time his form and pressure. Now this overdone, or come tardy off, though it make the unskillful laugh, cannot but make the judicious grieve; the censure of the which one must in your allowance o'erweigh a whole theatre of others. O, there be players that I have seen play, and heard others praise, and that highly, not to speak it profanely, that, neither having the accent of Christians nor the gait of Christian, pagan, nor man, have so strutted and bellowed that I have thought some of nature's journeymen had made men and not made them well, they imitated humanity so abominably.

First Player. I hope we have reformed that indifferently with us, sir.

Hamlet. O, reform it altogether. And let those that play your clowns speak no more than is set down for them; for there be of them that will themselves laugh, to set on some quantity of barren spectators to laugh too; though, in the mean time, some necessary question of the play be then to be considered: that's villainous, and shows a most pitiful ambition in the fool that uses it. Go, make you ready.

CHAPTER XIII
INTERVIEWS

"To be a well-favored man is the gift of fortune; but to write and read comes by nature."—SHAKESPEARE.

I. Introduction

For most of his material a reporter must rely upon his success as an interviewer. This, it has already been pointed out, requires courage, tact, persistence, and some knowledge of human nature. Its performance is beyond the powers of most boys and girls, and besides, if they tried it, they would annoy people. As a substitute, the exercises that follow have been devised. They involve interviews, it is true, but only with the members of a pupil's own family.

There are two ways to manage an interview. One may go directly at it, which is sometimes the best method, or one may approach the subject cautiously. It depends on the disposition of the person interviewed. The direct method will probably work well with mother, who is never out of sorts, but as to father—well, the case may be different; while sisters, brothers, cousins, aunts, and uncles present endless problems and opportunities.

Before interviewing anybody, it is a good plan always to write down the questions you wish to ask. But do not read them to the person interviewed. Get them so thoroughly into your own mind that you will forget none of them. As an exercise, make a set of questions such as you would need to ask in order to learn the facts contained in the following paragraphs from Franklin's *Autobiography*.

II. Assignments

Write the opening paragraphs of your own biography, covering the topics suggested below:

Week 1—My Ancestors.

Week 2—My Uncles.

Week 3—My Parents.

III. Model I

MY ANCESTORS

One of my uncles furnished me with several particulars relating to our ancestors. From his notes I learned that the family had lived in the same village, Ecton, in Northamptonshire, for three hundred years, and how much longer he knew not (perhaps from the time when the name of Franklin, that before was the name of an order of people, was assumed by them as a surname when others took surnames all over the kingdom), on a freehold of about thirty acres, aided by the smith's business, which had continued in the family until his time, the eldest son being always bred to that business, a custom which he and my father followed as to their eldest sons. When I searched the records of Ecton, I found an account of their births, marriages, and burials from the year 1555 only, there being no registers kept in that parish at any time preceding. By that register I perceived that I was the youngest son of the youngest son for five generations back. My grandfather Thomas, who was born in 1598, lived at Ecton till he grew too old to follow business longer, when he went to live with his son John, a dyer at Banbury, in Oxfordshire, with whom my father served an apprenticeship. There my grandfather died and lies buried. We saw his gravestone in 1758. His eldest son Thomas lived in the house at Ecton, and left it with the land to his only child, a daughter. My grandfather had four sons that grew up, viz: Thomas, John, Benjamin, and Josiah. I will give you what account I can of them.

[Page 79] IV. Queries

1. Who was Benjamin Franklin? Answer in a five-minute speech.
2. What is the difference between a biography and an autobiography?
3. Locate Ecton, Northamptonshire, Banbury, and Oxfordshire.
4. Point out all of the adjective phrases.
5. Does Franklin use simple, compound, or complex sentences, and in what proportion?
6. Make a list of the topics he discusses. Can you improve his order?
7. Are his sentences long or short?
8. Do they lack unity?
9. Can you find any metaphors or antitheses in the model?
10. Discuss the origin of the name Franklin. What is a surname? When did the English assume surnames?

V. Composition

Write an account of your own ancestors, choosing either your father's or your mother's family. Let the length be about the same as that of the model. The topics discussed should include the following:

1. Origin of surname.
2. European home.
3. Occupations.
4. My grandfather.
5. His sons.

Your father, mother, uncles, aunts, grandfathers, and grandmothers will furnish you with the material for your composition; and their aid may be supplemented by the books of genealogy that you will find in the public library. Remember that the items listed above were suggested to Franklin by his material; if you have interesting facts or traditions that cannot be included under the heads which he uses, put them in none the less. Matter should determine form.

VI. Model II

MY UNCLES

Thomas was bred a smith under his father; but, being ingenious, and encouraged in learning (as all my uncles were) by an Esquire, then the principal gentleman in that parish, he qualified himself for the business of scrivener; became a considerable man in the county; was a chief mover of all public-spirited undertakings for the county or town of Northampton, and his own village, of which many instances were related of him, and much taken notice of and patronized by the then Lord Halifax. He died in 1702, January 6, old style, just four years to a day before I was born. The account we received of his life and character from some old people at Ecton, I remember, struck you as something extraordinary. "Had he died on the same day," you said, "one might have supposed a transmigration."

John was bred a dyer, I believe, of woolens. Benjamin was bred a silk dyer, serving an apprenticeship at London. He was an ingenious man. I remember him well, for when he was a boy he came over to my father in Boston, and lived in the house with us for some years. He lived to a great age. His grandson, Samuel Franklin, now lives in Boston. He left behind him two quarto volumes, MS., of his own poetry, consisting of little occasional pieces addressed to his friends and relations. He had formed a shorthand of his own, which he taught me; but, never practicing it, I have now forgot it. I was named after this uncle, there being a particular affection between him and my father. He was very pious, a great attender of sermons of the best preachers, which he took down in his shorthand. He was also much of a politician.

VII. Topics for Oral Composition

1. What is an Esquire? A gentleman? A parish? A scrivener?
2. Explain the term "old style."
3. What is meant by transmigration?
4. What is an apprenticeship? An occasional piece?
5. Explain the terms "quarto," "folio," and "octavo."

VIII. Written Composition

Write an account of your uncles. Make it as rich as possible in concrete facts, for facts are the life and soul of composition. Let the length be about the same as that of the model. Note that Franklin discusses his uncles in an order determined by the principle that first and last places are the most conspicuous. He put the uncle about whom he knows most in last place, so as to have a strong ending, which grows, so to speak, to a climax; he puts the uncle who is entitled to second place first in order of discussion; and the uncle who is least important is mentioned in the middle.

IX. Model III

MY PARENTS

Josiah, my father, married young, and carried his wife with three children into New England about 1682. The conventicles having been forbidden by law and frequently disturbed induced some considerable men of his acquaintance to remove to that country, and he was prevailed with to accompany them thither, where they expected to enjoy their mode of religion with freedom. By the same wife he had four children more born there, and by a second wife ten more, in all seventeen, of whom I remember thirteen sitting at one time at his table, who all grew up to be men and women and married. I was the youngest son and the youngest child but two, and was born in Boston, New England. My mother, the second, was Abiah Folger, daughter of Peter Folger, one of the first settlers of New England, of whom honorable mention is made by Cotton Mather, in his church history of that country, as "a godly, pious, learned Englishman." I have heard that he wrote sundry small occasional pieces, but only one of them was printed, which I saw now many years since. It was written in 1675, in the home-spun verse of that time and people, and addressed to those then concerned in the government there. It was in favor of liberty of conscience and in behalf of the Baptists, [Page 82] Quakers, and other sectaries that had been under persecution. The whole appeared to me to be written with a good deal of decent plainness and manly freedom. The six concluding lines I remember, though I have forgotten the two first of the stanza; but the purport of them was that his censures proceeded from good will and therefore he would be known to be the author:

"Because to be a libeller

>   I hate it with my heart.
> From Sherburne town, where now I dwell,
>   My name I do put here;
> Without offence your real friend,
>   It is Peter Folgier!"

X. Questions and Topics for Oral Composition

1. What is the subject of "disturbed," line 3?
2. Discuss the subject of "conventicles."
3. To what religious sect did Josiah Franklin belong?
4. Why did he come to America?
5. Who was Cotton Mather?
6. Define "sundry" and "occasional."
7. What is "homespun verse"? Explain the figure.
8. Define "sectaries" and "stanza."

XI. Exercises

1. Rewrite Model III in modern English.
2. Write an account of your own parents of about the same length as Model III.
3. Before deciding finally on the style of this account of your parents, seek in the corresponding sections of several biographies for hints. Good ones may be discovered in Boswell's *Johnson*, Lockhart's *Scott*, Southey's *Nelson*, Trevelyan's *Macaulay*, and Hallam Tennyson's *Tennyson*.

XII. Suggested Reading

O. W. Holmes's *Grandmother's Story of Bunker Hill* and *Dorothy Q.*

XIII. Memorize

PROCRASTINATION

Be wise to-day; 'tis madness to defer;
Next day the fatal precedent will plead.
Procrastination is the thief of time.
At thirty, man suspects himself a fool;
Knows it at forty, and reforms his plan;
At fifty chides his infamous delay,
Pushes his prudent purpose to resolve,
In all the magnanimity of thought
Resolves, and re-resolves; then dies the same.
— EDWARD YOUNG.

CHAPTER XIV
THE EXPOSITION OF MECHANICS

*"'Tis not in mortals to command success.
But we'll do more, Sempronius; we'll deserve it."*
                                                JOSEPH ADDISON.

I. Assignments

1. Explain the plan of your own house.
2. Explain the plan of some new house that you pass on your way to school.
3. Explain the structure of a new locomotive, railway car, street car, automobile, ship, or aeroplane.
4. Explain the plan of your schoolhouse.
5. The papers contain many descriptions of new houses. These are usually written with a fine disregard of the laws of composition. Find and rewrite one of them. Do the same with a description of a ship such as is common in periodicals.

II. Model I

> The new suburban home of John Doe is located in a ten-acre tract on the northern side of the Seven-Mile Road, midway between Woodward Avenue and the Gratiot E. Turnpike. The material is reinforced concrete; the style, Colonial; the roof of green shingles; the size, 48 feet by 36 feet.
>
> From a front entrance porch a central hall 7 feet wide extends 29 feet to the rear of the house, terminating in a flight of stairs broken in the middle by a landing. Above

this landing a circular window gives plenty of light and at the same time forms a decorative feature.

[Page 85] On the right, as one enters the hall, is a room 9 feet by 14 feet, which may be used as a den or a reception room. Back of this is a living-room, 14 feet by 20 feet, with a fireplace at the rear end, and a French door that leads to a side piazza. This piazza, which is 20 feet by 7 feet, is covered and is equipped with sliding windows.

On the other side of the hall, in front, is the dining-room, 16 feet by 14 feet. This room has a fireplace, which faces the street, and a French door, which leads to a side porch 8 feet by 10. The latter is enclosed with glass and is used as a breakfast porch. Directly behind this porch is a small sewing-room, and, partly behind the sewing-room and partly behind the dining-room, is the kitchen, which is 12 feet square. In the northwest corner of the house, directly north of the sewing-room and west of the kitchen, are a small back porch and an entry large enough for a refrigerator. East of the kitchen, between it and the main hall, are a passage and service stairways leading to the cellar and the upper floors. The kitchen is thus separated from the rest of the house, either way, by two doors, which prevents the odors of the cooking from escaping.

The walls of the first floor are finished in oiled and waxed gumwood. The floors are oak, except in the kitchen, where hard pine is used.

On the second floor the rear of the space above the main hall is occupied by a passage, the front by a bathroom. On the eastern side of this passage, above the den, is a bedroom 16 feet by 14 feet, and back of this, above the living-room, a bedroom 14 feet by 11 feet. The latter has a fireplace in the north wall. On the western side of the passage, in front, above the dining-room, is the owner's chamber, 16 feet by 14 feet. From its southeast corner a door leads to the bathroom already mentioned; on its southwest side is a porch, and in its northern wall are two closets and a fireplace. In its rear a passage leads to a fourth chamber, 14 feet by 10 feet, which has an alcove, 9 feet by 8 feet. This alcove is directly above the sewing-room and the chamber is in the northwest corner of the house. Between it and the service stairway is a second bathroom.

On the third floor are three large chambers, an unfinished room for storage, and a servants' bath.

[Page 86] The cellar contains a laundry, a vegetable closet, coal-bins, and a hot-water heating-plant.

III. Analytical Discussion

1. Note the framework:
    a. "Four W's"—Par. 1.
    b. First Floor—
        Par. 2. Main Hall.
        Par. 3. Right Side.
        Par. 4. Left Side.
        Par. 5. Floors and Walls.
    c. Second Floor—Par. 6.
    d. Third Floor. Par. 7.
    e. Cellar—Par. 8.

2. *Words.* Define and explain the etymology of "suburban," "located," "reinforced," "concrete," "Colonial," "reception," "piazza," "porch," "refrigerator," "separated," "except," "servant," "closet," "effect."

3. *Sentences.* (*a*) Tell whether they are simple, complex, or compound. (*b*) Do any of them lack unity?

4. *Paragraphs.* (*a*) Can you find any violations of paragraph unity? (*b*) Observe that the following particulars are mentioned in Par. 1: location, material, shape, color, size. Is the same plan used in describing each room? In order to determine this, make a list of the items that are mentioned in explaining the construction of each.

5. *Transition.* Point out all of the transition words in the model.

6. *Figures of Speech.* Find a metaphor and an antithesis in the model.

IV. Model II

> The *Arizona* is the latest and greatest addition to the battle fleet of the United States.
>
> Her displacement is 31,400 tons, her length over all 600 feet, her maximum breadth 97 feet, and her draft under normal conditions 28 feet, 10 inches. Parsons's turbines of 29,000 horse-power give her a speed of 21 knots. Her fuel supply is 2322 tons of oil. She carries a crew of 1000 men. Her cost was $16,000,000.
>
> Her armament consists of twelve fourteen-inch and twenty-two five-inch guns, four three-pounders for the launches, two three-inch guns for salutes, and four twenty-two-inch torpedo tubes. The big guns are mounted in four turrets, two forward and two aft, each

containing three guns. The turrets nearer to the middle of the ship are enough higher than the forward and aft turrets to permit their guns to be fired directly ahead and astern respectively. This arrangement permits the concentration of six guns forward, six aft, and twelve on either broadside.

This vessel is probably armored more heavily than any other warship afloat. Her main belt is sixteen inches thick, while the *Iron Duke,* one of the latest British dreadnoughts, carries only twelve inches.

V. Notes and Queries

1. Observe the structure:
    Par. 1. General Description.
    Par. 2. Statistics.
    Par. 3. Offensive Power.
    Par. 4. Defensive Arrangements.
2. Could the same structure be used for the description of a freight boat, a passenger steamer, a ferryboat, a schooner, a sloop, a brig, a brigantine, a tugboat, a launch, a locomotive, a railway carriage, an airship, or an automobile?
3. What changes, if any, would you suggest?
4. Explain the terms "displacement," "draft," "normal," "knots," "pounds," "turrets."
5. Explain the metaphor in "belt." Is it a good one?

VI. Gathering Material

Do not get your material from reading; get it from observation. Don't steal it; earn it. Catch your fish; don't buy a string of dead ones at the fish-market, and then lie about the way you obtained them. Few of us can be original, but we can all be honest and industrious.

[Page 88] **VII. Organization**

Before you write, make a plan. It is as necessary in composition as in building. If the nature of your subject or the kind and quantity of your material render it desirable to deviate from the model, do not hesitate to do so. As a rule, however, it will be best to follow its plan rather closely. At all events, work from some plan. Don't get the idea that you can dash off a finished exposition in a few minutes.

VIII. Writing

Exposition above everything else should be clear. Say what you mean and mean what you say.

IX. Criticism

The written expositions of house plans may be tested by having the pupils exchange papers, and asking the recipients to draw the plans from the compositions.

X. Suggested Reading

Rudyard Kipling's *The Ship that Found Herself*.

XI. Memorize

CHARITY

Then gently scan your brother man,
   Still gentler sister woman;
Though they may gang a kennin' wrang,
   To step aside is human.

One point must still be greatly dark,
    The moving why they do it,
And just as lamely can ye mark
    How far perhaps they rue it.

[Page 89]
Who made the heart 'tis he alone
    Decidedly can try us;
He knows each chord—its various tone,
    Each spring—its various bias.
Then at the balance let's be mute;
    We never can adjust it;
What's done we partly may compute,
    But know not what's resisted.
Robert Burns.
←Contents

CHAPTER XV
THE EXPOSITION OF IDEAS

> "But words are things, and a small drop of ink,
> Falling like dew upon a thought, produces
> That which makes thousands, perhaps millions, think."
>
> LORD BYRON.

I. Introduction

THE exposition of ideas is difficult and important. It takes many forms, but only three can be noticed in this chapter: (1) Exposition through Narration; (2) Exposition through Condensation; (3) Exposition through Comparison. The three following models illustrate these three forms, respectively.

II. Model I

PUFFERS

The wise men of antiquity loved to convey instruction under the covering of apologue; and, though this practice is generally thought childish, we shall make no apology for adopting it on the present occasion. A generation which has bought eleven editions of a poem by Mr. Robert Montgomery may well condescend to listen to a fable of Pilpay.

A pious Brahmin, it is written, made a vow that on a certain day he would sacrifice a sheep, and on the appointed morning he went forth to buy one. There lived in his neighborhood three rogues who knew of his vow, and laid a scheme for profiting by it. The first met him and said, "Oh Brahmin, wilt thou buy a sheep? I have one fit for sacrifice." "It is for that very purpose," said the holy man, "that I came forth this day." Then the impostor opened a bag, and brought out of it an unclean beast, an ugly dog, lame and blind. Thereon the Brahmin cried out, "Wretch, who touchest things impure, and utterest things untrue, [Page 91] callest thou that cur a sheep?" "Truly," answered the other, "it is a sheep of the finest fleece and of the sweetest flesh. O Brahmin, it will be an offering most acceptable to the gods." "Friend," said the Brahmin, "either thou or I must be blind."

Just then one of the accomplices came up. "Praised be the gods," said this second rogue, "that I have been saved the trouble of going to the market for a sheep! This is such a sheep as I wanted. For how much wilt thou sell it?" When the Brahmin heard this his mind waved to and fro, like one swinging in the air at a holy festival. "Sir," said he to the newcomer, "take heed what thou dost; this is no sheep, but an unclean cur." "O Brahmin," said the newcomer, "thou art drunk or mad!"

At this time the third confederate drew near. "Let us ask this man," said the Brahmin, "what the creature is, and I will stand by what he shall say." To this the others agreed, and the Brahmin called out, "O stranger, what dost thou call this beast?" "Surely, O Brahmin," said the knave, "it is a fine sheep." Then the Brahmin said, "Surely the gods have taken away my senses"; and he asked pardon of him who carried the dog, and bought it for a measure of rice and a pot of ghee, and offered it up to the gods, who, being wroth at this unclean sacrifice, smote him with a sore disease in all his joints.

Thus, or nearly thus, if we remember rightly, runs the story of the Sanscrit Æsop. The moral, like the moral of every fable that is worth the telling, lies on the surface. The writer evidently means to caution us against the practices of puffers, a class of people who have more than once talked the public into the most absurd errors, but who surely never played a more curious or a more difficult trick than when they passed Mr. Robert Montgomery off upon the world as a great poet.—Thomas Babington Macaulay, *Essay on Mr. Robert Montgomery's Poems.*

III. Topics for Discussion

1. The Fable, which is here illustrated, is a simple story told to point a moral or to make clear a complicated situation. Æsop and George Ade are perhaps the most [Page 92] interesting authors of fables—at least to twentieth-century Americans. An entertaining program may be arranged by assigning each member of the class a fable of one of these writers for oral reporting. The model illustrates well the value of the fable form in newspaper exposition.

2. Note the paragraph structure: (1) Introduction; (2) "Four W's," or Situation 1; (3) Climax, or Situation 2; (4) Dénouement, Result, or Situation 3; (5) Moral, or Point.

3. Define and discuss the etymology of "antiquity," "apologue," "apology," "edition," "fable," "impostor," "accomplice," "confederate," "knave," "ghee," "caution," "puffers."

4. What proportion of Macaulay's words in Paragraphs 2, 3, and 4 are monosyllables and dissyllables? Does he here use more or fewer big words in proportion than in Paragraphs 1 and 5? What is the effect on his style?

VIII. Suggested Reading

Cæsar's *Commentaries on the Gallic War*. Macaulay's *Frederick the Great*. Southey's *Life of Nelson*. Parkman's *The Conspiracy of Pontiac*. Parkman's *Montcalm and Wolfe*. Fiske's *The Mississippi Valley in the Civil War*.

IX. Memorize

HUMANITY

I would not enter on my list of friends,
Though graced with polished manners and fine sense,
Yet wanting sensibility, the man
Who needlessly sets foot upon a worm.
An inadvertent step may crush the snail
That crawls at evening in the public path;
But he that has humanity, forewarned,
Will tread aside and let the reptile live.
The creeping vermin, loathsome to the sight,
And charged perhaps with venom, that intrudes,
A visitor unwelcome, into scenes
Sacred to neatness and repose, the alcove,
The chamber, or refectory, may die;
A necessary act incurs no blame.
Not so when, held within their proper bounds,
And guiltless of offence, they range the air,
Or take their pastime in the spacious field.
There they are privileged; and he that hunts
Or harms them there is guilty of a wrong.
The sum is this: If man's convenience, health,
Or safety interfere, his rights and claims
Are paramount, and must extinguish theirs.
Else they are all—the meanest things that are—

As free to live and to enjoy that life,
As God was free to form them at the first,
Who, in his sovereign wisdom, made them all.
Ye, therefore, who love mercy, teach your sons
To love it too.
                               WILLIAM COWPER.

CHAPTER XVI
EDITORIALS—CONSTRUCTIVE

"Opinion in good men is but knowledge in the making."

JOHN MILTON.

I. Introduction

An editorial is a newspaper article in which the opinions of the editor are set forth. News deals with fact. In news articles the opinion of the writer must be suppressed. The pronouns "I" and "we" have no place in news. The essence of the editorial, on the other hand, is the opinion of the writer. On the editorial page, the man who directs the policy of a paper seeks to interpret the news in accordance with his own views and to persuade the public to adopt those views.

Editorials are therefore for the most part argumentative. In them the writer either comments directly on some news item and thus produces what may be called a constructive editorial, or takes issue with the editorial opinion of a rival in a controversial editorial, his object being to destroy the sentiment produced by his rival's article.

The power of the editorial writer for good or for evil is clear. That it is usually exerted for good is one of the best evidences that the newspapers of the country are controlled by men who desire to serve the public well.

II. Assignments

1. Write an editorial calling attention to some feature of current news.
2. Write an editorial advocating some plan or reform for the good of city, state, nation, or mankind.

III. Model I

We made the point some months ago that our electric light companies have been far behind those of Europe in making it possible for poor people to get their service. It is interesting to note that the Indiana and Michigan Electric Company, which operates in South Bend, Ind. (plows, wagons, sewing-machines), has started a campaign to do just this thing. About a third of the inhabitants of South Bend are laborers from Poland, Austria, and the Balkan countries, whose wages average about $1.50 or $1.75 per day. The electric company has figured out plans whereby houses can be wired at a cost of from $9 to $15 each, and lighting service can be given for a minimum of $1 per month. A Polish sales agent has been hired to talk to the newcomers, write advertisements for their papers, and attend to their complaints—in short, to translate electricity into Slovak, etc. The men engaged in the work are confident of success and are going after it. The effect in giving these people better ways and standards of living, in getting them a share in our modern American civilization, and a feeling that they are so sharing will necessarily be very great. This is solid public service, and it is far better than any charity. What is being done on this problem in your town?—*Collier's Weekly*, November 28, 1914.[10]

IV. Comments and Exercises

1. This is a constructive editorial with just a hint of argument. Find the argument.
2. Note the framework of the paragraph: (Sentence 1) Topic; (Sentence 2—Sentence 6) Story; (Sentence 7) Conclusion.
3. Find the "Four W's."

4. Remember that the perfect tense denotes an act begun in the past and completed in the present. Does its use sufficiently tell when a thing is or was done?

5. Write a similar editorial commenting on some improvement in your own town.

V. Model II

> Were we suddenly called upon to face a crisis such as Europe was called upon to face with but very little warning, it would find us wofully unprepared. In the security of our peace we have neglected to build up an organization capable of performing the multitudinous services of war, or of any great disaster, either political or physical, which may come into a nation's life. The thousands of young men in colleges and universities offer a field for the development of such a force of trained men in a way that would entirely revolutionize our educational as well as our defensive system.
>
> As our athletics are conducted to-day, a few picked men have trainers, coaches, rubbers, and waiters for the purpose of preparing them for a conflict with a correspondingly small group of similarly trained men from other institutions. The remainder of the student body, which makes this training possible, is meanwhile physically utterly neglected.
>
> Yet the average young man entering college is quite as much in need of physical development and training as of mental. The country, too, is in need of disciplined, trained men; and this double need can be met—can be met for less money than is expended on a single season's football team. A system of military drill, under the supervision of experts in military discipline and

hygiene, with the coöperation of the athletic associations of the colleges, and under the auspices of the United States Government, would prove of inestimable value to every student in the college, and would furnish to the nation a groundwork upon which a magnificent national service could be established. A spirit of true patriotism and of unselfish public service would be instilled in the students. The nucleus of a trained military corps would be established from which officers and men could be recruited with but little additional training in time of war.—*Puck*.11

[Page 100] **VI. Comments and Exercises**

1. What is the point of this editorial?
2. Note the point of each paragraph: (Par. 1) Our colleges might furnish the means of remedying our national lack of preparation for war; (Par. 2) at present our athletics benefit only a few individuals; (Par. 3) if military training were introduced into our colleges, it would benefit both individuals and the nation.
3. A more logical arrangement would be: (Par. 1) The United States is not prepared for war; (Par. 2) as now organized, our college athletics benefit only a few individuals; (Par. 3) if military training were introduced into our colleges, individual students and the nation alike would be benefited.
4. In which arrangement is paragraph unity better observed?
5. Is the arrangement in the model better in any respect than the one suggested?
6. The following words are hackneyed: "wofully," "utterly," "inestimable," "magnificent," "groundwork." Suggest some synonyms. Can any of these words be omitted? Lowell's rule was:

"Cut out the adjectives and adverbs. Make the nouns and verbs do the work."

7. Explain the construction of "with but very little warning," "for the purpose," "from other institutions," "physically," "utterly," "drill."

8. What is the difference between "development" and "training"? Between "true patriotism" and "unselfish public service"? "College" and "university"?

9. Does this model contain any misstatements of fact?

10. Is the plan feasible or desirable?

11. Could it be extended to secondary schools?

12. Find in the model at least four mixed metaphors. If you do not know what a mixed metaphor is, perhaps this classic example of one will inform you: "Mr. Speaker, I smell a rat. I see him brewing in the air. But, mark me, I shall yet nip him in the bud."

13. Discuss the meaning and etymology of "crisis," "disaster," "political," "physical," "nation," "revolutionize," "educational," "athletics," "institutions," "disciplined," [Page 101] "military," "supervision," "experts," "auspices," "spirit," "instilled," "nucleus," "corps," "recruited," "additional."

14. Shall we say "instilled in," "instilled into," or "developed in"?

15. Write an answer to Model II.

16. The great merits of Model II lie in its content and its construction. The fundamental principle on which it is built might be called the "killing-two-birds-with-one-stone idea." Two things are wrong; one reform will make both right. Can you think of any other subject which might be discussed on the same principle?

VII. Suggested Reading

Lamb's *Dissertation on Roast Pig*. Addison's *Hilpa and Shalum*. Emerson's *Compensation*. Holmes's *The Broomstick Train*.

VIII. Memorize

METRICAL FEET[12]

Trōchee̅ | trĭps frŏm | lōng tŏ | shōrt ‖;
Frōm lōng | tō lōng | ĭn sōl|ĕmn sōrt
Slōw Spōn|dee̅ stālks; ‖ strōng foōt, yĕt | īll ăblĕ
Ēvĕr tŏ | kee̅p ŭp wĭth | Dāctȳl trĭ|sȳllăblĕ;
Ĭām|bŭs mōves | frŏm shōrt | tŏ lōng;
Wĭth ă lea̅p | ănd ă boūnd | thĕ swĭft Ān|ăpĕsts thrōng.
　　　　　SAMUEL TAYLOR COLERIDGE.

[Alternative formats.]
← Contents

CHAPTER XVII
EDITORIALS—DESTRUCTIVE

> "O great corrector of enormous times,
> Shaker of o'er-rank states, thou grand decider
> Of dusty and old titles, that healest with blood
> The earth when it is sick, and curest the world
> O' the pleurisy of people!"
>
> — BEAUMONT AND FLETCHER.

I. Introduction

IN Chapter XVI constructive editorials were discussed. The object of this chapter is to present a few exercises on destructive editorials. Their object, of course, is not really to create ruin; it is merely to clear away rubbish in order to prepare the ground for the edifice of truth.

II. Assignment

Write an editorial in reply to an editorial in which a false position is assumed by the writer.

III. Model I

> Vice-President Marshall's declaration, made some time ago at Wabash College, that the old man is being shoved off the stage everywhere, needs revision, as does the opinion of another statesman that men over fifty are atrophied.
>
> In the last great war between France and Germany the campaign was planned and led by elderly men. The Emperor William, then King of Prussia, was in his seventy-fourth year; Von Moltke, the master strategist

of the war, was seventy-one years old; General von Roon was sixty-eight; and Bismarck, the master mind in the larger field, was in his fifty-sixth year.

In the next great war in which high military efficiency [Page 103] was displayed, Admiral Togo was approaching his sixtieth year when he took the field; Prince Oyama, the commander-in-chief of the Japanese forces in Manchuria, had passed his sixtieth year; Field Marshal Nodzu was sixty-three; Field Marshal Yamagata was sixty-six; General Kuroki was sixty; and General Nogi, who took Port Arthur after a series of desperate conflicts, carried on with unflinching energy and almost breathless rapidity, was nearly sixty years of age.

In the present war Lord Kitchener, the organizing genius of the English army, is sixty-four; and Sir John French, commanding the English forces in the field, is sixty-two. When Lord Roberts was sent to South Africa to snatch victory out of defeat, he was sixty-eight years of age.

On the French side, General Joffre is sixty-two; General Pau is sixty-six; General Castelnau, the third in command, is well advanced in the sixties; and General Gallieni, who is in command of the defenses of Paris, is seventy.

The German armies are also led by a group of elderly men. Count von Huelsenberg has reached the mature age of seventy-eight; Field Marshal von der Goltz is seventy-one; General von Kluck has reached his sixty-eighth year; General von Emmich was sixty-six; and General von Hindenberg is sixty-seven.

These figures suggest that, while fifty may be the deadline among Democratic statesmen, it appears to be a kind of life-line among great leaders abroad.—Adapted from *The Outlook*, November 11, 1914.13

IV. Analysis

Observe the framework. Paragraph 1 states the point to be proved. Paragraphs 2–5 are composed of examples, arranged thus:

1. The War of 1871.
2. The War of 1905.
3. The Present War.
   a. France.
   b. England.
   c. Germany.

[Page 104] The order, in other words, is at once the order of chronology and that of climax, which combine to make the facts easy to remember. Paragraph 6 summarizes the argument and clinches it by a sharp antithesis.

V. Exercises

1. Using a similar framework, write an editorial disproving by examples the point made by the writer of the model.
2. Write an editorial proving by examples any proposition which you believe to be true and in which you are deeply interested.
3. Prove or disprove by example any one of the following propositions:
   a. Left-hand batters are better than right-hand batters.
   b. Germans are better ball-players than Irishmen.

c. Frenchmen cannot play ball.

d. Men write better than women.

e. Asphalt pavements are more durable than brick pavements.

f. Germany has contributed more to the world's culture than England.

g. College graduates are more successful as statesmen than are self-made men.

h. Very tall men have ever very empty heads.

i. Athletes usually succeed well in after life.

j. Dr. Samuel Johnson was a great wit. (For Johnson, substitute, if you wish, Geoffrey Chaucer, William Shakespeare, Francis Bacon, Samuel Butler, Alexander Pope, Charles Lamb, Sidney Smith, Oliver Wendell Holmes, James Russell Lowell, or Mark Twain.)

In the model there are twenty-two examples. In your composition there must be at least ten.

VI. Model II

WHAT DOES A MAN PRODUCE?

Among the banners of the unemployed in New York when they came in collision with the police was one reading, "We Want All We Produce."

[Page 105] There is a common impression among Socialistic workmen, encouraged by some of the new-fangled college professors, that the weaver produces all the cloth that comes off the loom he tends, and he is robbed if his wages are only a part of the value of the cloth. But he is only one of a long line of producers, each of whom has to get some of the money for which that cloth is sold.

There was a farmer who grew the raw fiber. There was a railroad that transported the fiber. There was a long list of workmen who did various things in the preparation of that fiber. It took several classes of men to convert that fiber into yarn. Some men dug the coal and a railroad hauled it. It took a good many men a considerable time to build the loom and the engine and the mill, and all of them have got to be paid. The men who have paid all these previous classes of workers may reimburse themselves out of a part of the proceeds of the bolt of cloth without committing any robbery. What are the dividends but the reimbursement of the people that have paid the miners and mechanics and builders for their work before the cloth was sold?

The report of the Comptroller of the Currency shows that the average return on all the shares and bonds of all the corporations in the United States is 4.3 per cent. That doesn't look unreasonable. It isn't very much more than savings-bank interest. Of course, some corporations make very much more, but many must make nothing in order to bring the average down to 4.3 per cent. Besides, there are a few bonds that do not pay 4.5 per cent or more, so that the average return on the shares, which represent the ownership of the mills and factories, would be less than 4.3 per cent.

What does a man produce? Well, put a man with only his bare hands upon a spot of earth, or in a mine hole, or by the side of a stream and how much will he produce? What are the chances that he will not starve to death before he can produce anything? If you give him tools, and "grub-stake" him, in mining lingo, or support him until he has produced something and it has been marketed, the produce of other men has been given him. They have got to be paid for their produce in some way. The man in question can't have all he produces without defrauding the men who produced [Page 106] the tools and food which he used during the time he was getting his product made or extracted.14—*Philadelphia Record.*

VII. Analysis

1. What is proved by this editorial?
2. The method of Model I consists of overwhelming the enemy with an avalanche of examples. The method of Model II is to define the words used by an opponent and, by analyzing the meaning of what he asserts, to prove that he does not see his way through the question.
3. Note the framework: (Par. 1) "Four W's"; (Par. 2) Statement of Positions of Opponent and Writer; (Par. 3) Exposition of Writer's Position; (Par. 4) Refutation of Opponent's Idea; (Par. 5) Conclusion.

VIII. Exercises

1. Define and discuss the etymology of "collision," "transported," "convert," "considerable," "reimburse," "dividend," "corporations," "factories," "starve," "lingo," "support," "extract," "percentage," "average."
2. Subject for short expository speeches: "Socialism," "Shares," "Bonds," "Corporations," "Savings Banks," "Interest."
3. Write an answer to the model.
4. Write an editorial refuting some current fallacy or what you deem such. Use the analytic method of the model.

5. Examine the editorials in some current paper to determine whether they are expository or argumentative, constructive or destructive, if their frameworks are as good as those of the models, if their matter is as convincing, if their style is as good, and if their total effect is better or worse.

IX. Suggested Reading

Thomas Gray's *Elegy in a Country Churchyard*.

X. Memorize

[Page 107] **OLD IRONSIDES**[15]

Ay, tear her tattered ensign down!
   Long has it waved on high,
And many an eye has danced to see
   That banner in the sky;
Beneath it rung the battle shout,
   And burst the cannon's roar;—
The meteor of the ocean air
   Shall sweep the clouds no more.

Her deck, once red with heroes' blood,
   Where knelt the vanquished foe,
When winds were hurrying o'er the flood
   And waves were white below,
No more shall feel the victor's tread,
   Or know the conquered knee;—
The harpies of the shore shall pluck
   The eagle of the sea!

Oh, better that her shattered hulk
   Should sink beneath the wave;
Her thunders shook the mighty deep,

And there should be her grave;
Nail to the mast her holy flag,
  Set every threadbare sail,
And give her to the god of storms,
  The lightning and the gale.
                OLIVER WENDELL HOLMES.

CHAPTER XVIII
ADVERTISEMENTS

"I hold every man a debtor to his profession; from the which as men of course do seek to receive countenance and profit, so ought they of duty to endeavour themselves by way of amends to be a help and ornament thereunto."—FRANCIS BACON.

I. Introduction

IN no field is the writer of English more generously rewarded than in advertising. The annual expenditure for advertising in the United States is close to $1,000,000,000 and is rapidly increasing. Writers skilled in presenting goods to the public command very large salaries in the distribution of this great sum. The profession has been steadily attaining higher standards and has made a place for its members in nearly every business house in the country. It is certain, however, that there is still a vast field open for advertising development.

II. Assignment I

Make a list of the reasons that would induce you to buy a particular kind of fountain pen; suit of clothes; set of books; stove or range; lead pencil; candy.

III. Example

(See page 109.)

IV. Definition

An advertisement is an argumentative composition cut down to its simplest elements, a composition in which single words represent sentences or even paragraphs of ordinary writing. A sentence in an advertisement frequently conveys the meaning that in ordinary writing would be expanded into a long descriptive essay. The principles of composition-writing apply to advertising in the superlative degree. Above all things else, an advertisement must be clear, coherent, and forceful. In addition to these things it must be brief.

[Page 109] **Model Shoes**

   make happy, handsome feet.

Model Shoes

   are made on natural foot-fitting lasts and feel right the first time.

Model Shoes

   are made of carefully selected hides tanned by the special process which increases their wearing quality thirty per cent. Every operation from cutting to final packing is under the supervision of experts who are specially trained in their line.

Model Shoes

   are designed by shoe artists who watch every turn in the smart productions of fashionable New York and London bootmakers and combine the most favored lines with *model*

> comfort into distinctive *model* designs.
>
> $4.50 at your store
> *Write for Style Booklet*
>
> **Model Shoemakers**
> **Lowell, Mass.**

V. Assignment II

From the reasons that you have listed in Assignment I, pick out the one that most attracts you in the case of each of the articles named. Give a reason for your choice. Find a quality in each article that you especially desire but rarely find.

VI. Forcefulness in Advertising

An advertisement must first of all demand and win attention. The first word, the first sentence, must be strong enough to arrest the eye of the average reader, who runs hastily through the advertising matter of a magazine, newspaper, or other medium. It must catch the reader's interest, and hold his attention long enough to lead him into the remainder of the argument.

So far as possible the first sentence, in some cases the first word, should contain the heart of the message, the one big thing that you have to say about the article you have to advertise. If you fail to get your reader's interest with your first sentence, the word or words that attracted his attention to your advertisement, you have lost him forever. You will have no opportunity to present to him the argument that may follow. Your attention words are read by your maximum audience. Your most attractive argument in its most striking form should therefore be presented to them at once.

VII. Assignment III

Write a sentence presenting the arguments selected in Assignment II in the strongest and most attractive sentences that you can devise. Reduce the sentences to the single words that express the ideas most vividly.

VIII. Humor in Advertising

As an attention feature, a touch of humor is valuable in advertising. It tends to put the reader into a pleasant frame of mind, a frame of mind in which he is likely to listen more attentively to what you have to say. It operates in the same way as the funny story that usually prefaces the remarks of the after-dinner speaker. The humor, however, must have a direct and unmistakable bearing on the body of your advertising. Irrelevant humor is as much a waste of valuable advertising space as an irrelevant illustration. Advertising space costs too much to be used for anything but advertising. Grotesque illustrations and far-fetched puns are no longer found in advertising columns, because they have been found ineffective.

IX. Illustrations

In advertising practice the attention feature is frequently supplied by an illustration showing the article advertised in the use that is emphasized in the body of the advertisement, or in a way to illustrate the special argument presented. The importance of the attention factor is indicated by the large amount of [Page 112] space that is occupied by such illustrations. Some experiments have indicated, however, that a well-written attention line is fully as effective as an average illustration.

X. Suggested Reading

Carl Schurz's *Life of Abraham Lincoln*.

XI.

IPHIGENEIA AND AGAMEMNON

Iphigeneia, when she heard her doom
At Aulis, and when all beside the king
Had gone away, took his right hand, and said:
"O father! I am young and very happy.
I do not think the pious Calchas heard
Distinctly what the goddess spake; old age
Obscures the senses. If my nurse, who knew
My voice so well, sometimes misunderstood,
While I was resting on her knee both arms,
And hitting it to make her mind my words,
And looking in her face, and she in mine,
Might not he, also, hear one word amiss,
Spoken from so far off, even from Olympus?"
The father placed his cheek upon her head,
And tears dropt down it; but the king of men
Replied not. Then the maiden spake once more:
"O father! sayest thou nothing? Hearest thou not
Me, whom thou ever hast, until this hour,
Listened to fondly, and awakened me
To hear my voice amid the voice of birds,
When it was inarticulate as theirs,
And the down deadened it within the nest?"
He moved her gently from him, silent still;
And this, and this alone, brought tears from her,
Although she saw fate nearer. Then with sighs:
"I thought to have laid down my hair before
Benignant Artemis, and not dimmed
Her polished altar with my virgin blood;
I thought to have selected the white flowers
To please the nymphs, and to have asked of each
By name, and with no sorrowful regret,
Whether, since both my parents willed the change
I might at Hymen's feet bend my clipt brow;

And (after these who mind us girls the most)
Adore our own Athene, that she would
Regard me mildly with her azure eyes,—
But, father, to see you no more, and see
Your love, O father! go ere I am gone!"
Gently he moved her off, and drew her back,
Bending his lofty head far over hers;
And the dark depths of nature heaved and burst.
He turned away,—not far, but silent still.
She now first shuddered; for in him, so nigh,
So long a silence seemed the approach of death,
And like it. Once again she raised her voice:
"O father! if the ships are now detained,
And all your vows move not the gods above,
When the knife strikes me there will be one prayer
The less to them; and purer can there be
Any, or more fervent, than the daughter's prayer
For her dear father's safety and success?"
A groan that shook him shook not his resolve.
An aged man now entered, and without
One word stepped slowly on, and took the wrist
Of the pale maiden. She looked up, and saw
The fillet of the priest and calm, cold eyes.
Then turned she where her parent stood, and cried:
"O father! grieve no more; the ships can sail."

     WALTER SAVAGE LANDOR.[16]

       ←Contents

[Page 114] CHAPTER XIX
ADVERTISEMENTS (*continued*)

"Discretion of speech is more than eloquence; and to speak agreeably to him with whom we deal is more than to speak in good words or in good order."—Francis Bacon.

I. Assignment I

Clip from current newspapers or magazines five advertisements which in your opinion have effective attention lines. Pick out five advertisements which in your opinion have ineffective attention lines. Give your reasons for your choice.

II. Assignment II

a. Taking the attention arguments selected in the preceding chapter, set down all the questions that you might ask as a possible customer if you had been attracted by the attention line.

b. In the five examples of effective advertising selected from newspapers or magazines, set down the questions that are answered in the matter following the attention lines.

III. Coherence in Advertising

An effective advertisement must be a logically developed argument leading from the attraction of attention to the point where the reader is convinced that he wants your goods, and beyond that to the point where he will take some definite physical action to get them.

[Page 115] The steps intervening between attention and action may be sketched in the briefest terms, may in some exceptional cases be omitted entirely from the final form of the advertisement, but must be carefully worked out in the mind of the writer, no step being omitted that is essential in the chain of reasoning that the ordinary mind must follow.

Obviously the chain of reasoning must start from the attention line. If you have attracted your reader by saying "Prices Cut," you must tell him how much the reduction is and why you have made the reduction. If, on the other hand, you have attracted the attention by saying "Our Goods are the Best," you must explain the reasons why they are the best. That the mind of the reader may be held to the line of the argument from attention to action, all material that has no bearing upon this line of argument must be excluded.

IV. Exercise

Answer the questions about the various articles set down in Assignment I, being careful to follow the logical order in which they would occur and to exclude all material that does not relate directly to the argument you have selected.

V. Clinching Results

When you have attracted the attention of your reader and carried him along through a logical argument to the conviction that he wants your goods, one thing more remains. He must be induced to act upon his conviction. Up to this point his part has been passive; he has been asked merely to sit in his easy chair and read what you have to say. Now he must be [Page 116] aroused to activity; he must be brought to the point of putting on his hat and coat and going out to buy your goods. The strongest language form at our command is required here, the direct urgent imperative. Involuntarily people tend to obey orders that are given them. The appeal must, of course, be courteous, so as not to offend; but it must be strong enough to induce action. Compare the strength of "Sign here for free booklet" with "If you will sign on this line, we will send you our free booklet."

When your reader has been aroused to action, his way should be made as easy as possible. Every direction that he may need should be plainly before him, every convenience that will reduce his action to a minimum. He should be told clearly how and where he can get the goods that you have convinced him he wants, your name, your address, your telephone number, and everything else that will enable him to reach you promptly and certainly.

VI. Assignment III

Write a compelling sentence for each of the advertisements constructed in Assignment II (*a*), adding the necessary conclusion.

Construct a series of five advertisements, each dealing with a single attractive feature of one of the articles selected in the preceding work. Each advertisement should carry its argument through from attention to action.

VII. Suggested Reading

James Parton's *Captains of Industry*.

[Page 117] ## VIII. Memorize

THE PULLEY

When God at first made man,
Having a glass of blessing standing by;
Let us (said he) pour on him all we can:
Let the world's riches which dispersed lie
    Contract into a span.

So strength first made a way;
Then beauty flow'd, then wisdom, honour, pleasure;
When almost all was out, God made a stay,
Perceiving that alone, of all his treasure,
    Rest in the bottom lay.

    For if I should (said he)
Bestow this jewel also on my creature,
He would adore my gifts instead of me,
And rest in Nature, not the God of Nature;
    So both should losers be.

    Yet let him keep the rest,
But keep them with repining restlessness:
Let him be rich and weary, that at least,
If goodness lead him not, yet weariness
    May toss him to my breast.

GEORGE HERBERT.

CHAPTER XX
ADVERTISEMENTS (*concluded*)

"Honesty is the best policy."

BENJAMIN FRANKLIN.

I. Assignment I

PICK out in a large advertisement for a breakfast food the number of words of one syllable other than prepositions or articles; the words of two syllables; of three syllables; of more than three syllables. Reduce your results to percentages.

Make a similar study of advertisements for a set of books, of chewing gum, of an automobile, and of a piece of machinery in some technical publication. Compare results with a similar count in a newspaper paragraph, an encyclopedia paragraph, and paragraphs from Macaulay, Dickens, Carlyle, and Kipling.

II. Clearness

Clear, simple language, language that will be readily understood by the least intelligent of your possible customers, is an essential of good advertising. Every word that is above the lowest reasonable level of understanding limits the number of possible customers. The railroad attorney who was asked to write a notice that would warn people to be careful at railroad crossings did not dig into his law books for a polysyllabic sentence like this: "Whereas this is the intersection of a public highway with the right-of-way of the —— Railroad Corporation, each and every individual is hereby advised to exercise extreme caution." He wrote a sentence which is a classic in its way "Stop! Look! Listen! Railroad Crossing."

III. Assignment II

In the advertisements selected for Assignment I, count the number of words in each sentence and strike an average for each. Make a comparison with sentence length in other writings as suggested.

IV. Adaptation to Audience

The degree to which the simplification of language in an advertisement should be carried depends upon the audience addressed. It is evident that a larger and less educated portion of the public is included in the possible customers for breakfast food and chewing gum than there are in the portion who would be likely to purchase a set of books. An even smaller portion of the public would be interested in an automobile or a piece of automatic machinery. A good advertisement should be framed in language that will be understood by all possible purchasers of an article. Many household articles, such as bread, breakfast food, candy, and confections, are advertised in language that a fourth-grade child will readily understand.

V. Assignment III

Write an advertisement for an athletic contest in which your school will take part, addressing it to the students in your school.
Write an advertisement to introduce a new candy or confection among grammar-school children.
Write an advertisement for boys' hats; for girls' hats; for overalls; for a magazine devoted to automobiles; for a magazine devoted to fiction.

VI. Simplicity in Structure

An advertisement must be clear, not only in language and construction, but in mechanical structure as well. Attention-lines and command-lines must be short and set up so as to stand out clearly from the body of the advertisement. The eye takes in automatically from four to six words at a glance, setting the natural limit of length for strong features in an advertisement. Artistic arrangement helps an advertisement because carefully balanced matter is more attractive than inartistic combinations. A well-balanced advertisement, an advertisement in which the points are properly subordinated, conveys its meaning to the reader more easily than a badly distributed statement of the same arguments. In the last analysis good art is little more than good order, order that is pleasing to the eye as well as the mind. Good order requires a distribution of eye-effects that coincides with the distribution of mind effects.

VII. Assignment IV

Measure ten particularly attractive advertisements, illustrated or otherwise. Find the line on which the attention is focused and measure its distance from the top and bottom. Test these distances by the formulæ:

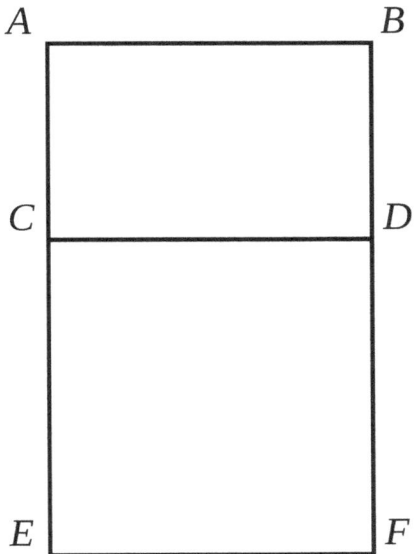

a. *AB* = 1 inch.
   AC = .62 inch.
   AE = 1.62 inches.

b. *AE* : *AB* :: *AE* + *AB* : *AE*
   1.62 : 1 :: 2.62 : 1.62

c. *CD* : *AC* :: *CD* + *AC* : *AD*
   1 : .62 :: 1.62 : 1

[Page 121] This is the so-called "golden rectangle," the most pleasing of all rectangular forms. The attention-line *CD* is at the point that makes the upper section a "golden rectangle." The capital letter "H" is also one of the most common arrangements in advertising. The square is another pleasing figure and there are many other forms in which advertising matter may be balanced.

VIII. Brevity

Advertising occupies space for which a high rate frequently is paid. Brief statement is therefore a factor of great importance. If a small space is all that is available, the problem of attracting attention becomes most important. It should be evident that a few words clearly and plainly printed are far more effective in a small space than a long message that is in such fine print that it will strain the eyes of the reader. In the one case you say something at least to your reader. In the other, you have no chance to say anything because you have tried to say too much. When it is necessary to confine your message to a small space, the attention-sentence, or in some cases the command-sentence, is the part to use. Many signs seen from the rapidly moving window of a street-car or railroad train carry only the name of the product attractively displayed, with a command to use it.

IX. Assignment V

Select one of the articles for which you have written advertising and write a complete advertising campaign for it, including five newspaper advertisements, five magazine advertisements, a four-page folder for distribution, signs for street-cars, signs for posting [Page 122] along highways, and other devices that you think would be effective.

X. Classified Advertisements

Most newspapers carry columns of classified advertising consisting of many small advertisements grouped together under various heads. These are commonly used by the public for getting help; obtaining situations; buying, selling, and renting real estate; and disposing of miscellaneous articles. The principles of advertising compositions apply also to these advertisements. The attention-factor is not so important, however, as the reader of the advertisements in the classified columns is looking for the article or service that you to have sell. A glance through the classified columns of a newspaper will show clearly the increased attractiveness resulting from the skillful arrangement of details and the use of clear forceful words.

www.ingramcontent.com/pod-product-compliance
Lightning Source LLC
Chambersburg PA
CBHW081114080526
44587CB00021B/3592